T0383948

# Cambridge Elements ☰

Elements in Psychology and Culture
edited by
Kenneth D. Keith
*University of San Diego*

# THE UNIVERSALITY OF EMOTION

## *Perspectives from the Sciences and Humanities*

Bradley J. Irish
*Arizona State University*

CAMBRIDGE
UNIVERSITY PRESS

Shaftesbury Road, Cambridge CB2 8EA, United Kingdom

One Liberty Plaza, 20th Floor, New York, NY 10006, USA

477 Williamstown Road, Port Melbourne, VIC 3207, Australia

314–321, 3rd Floor, Plot 3, Splendor Forum, Jasola District Centre,
New Delhi – 110025, India

103 Penang Road, #05–06/07, Visioncrest Commercial, Singapore 238467

Cambridge University Press is part of Cambridge University Press & Assessment,
a department of the University of Cambridge.

We share the University's mission to contribute to society through the pursuit of
education, learning and research at the highest international levels of excellence.

www.cambridge.org
Information on this title: www.cambridge.org/9781009565714

DOI: 10.1017/9781009442534

First published 2025

*A catalogue record for this publication is available from the British Library*

ISBN 978-1-009-56571-4 Hardback
ISBN 978-1-009-44251-0 Paperback
ISSN 2515-3986 (online)
ISSN 2515-3943 (print)

Cambridge University Press & Assessment has no responsibility for the persistence
or accuracy of URLs for external or third-party internet websites referred to in this
publication and does not guarantee that any content on such websites is, or will
remain, accurate or appropriate.

# The Universality of Emotion

## Perspectives from the Sciences and Humanities

Elements in Psychology and Culture

DOI: 10.1017/9781009442534
First published online: January 2025

Bradley J. Irish
*Arizona State University*

**Author for correspondence**: Bradley J. Irish, bradley.irish@asu.edu

**Abstract:** This Element surveys how a number of major disciplines – psychology, neuroscience, sociology, anthropology, philosophy, history, linguistics, and literary/cultural studies – have addressed the long-standing research question of whether human emotions should be thought of as meaningfully "universal." The Element presents both the universalist and anti-universalist positions, and concludes by considering attempts to move beyond this increasingly unhelpful binary.

**Keywords:** emotion, universality, constructed emotion theory, basic emotion theory, biocultural approaches

ISBNs: 9781009565714 (HB) 9781009442510 (PB), 9781009442534 (OC)
ISSNs: 2515-3986 (online), 2515-3943 (print)

# Contents

# Introduction

In virtually all scholarly traditions that analyze emotion, researchers have historically been divided on a fundamental question: Should human emotions be understood as meaningfully "universal"? While most scholars today, speaking informally, would probably acknowledge that there are both universal and culturally particular elements to human emotional experience, the fact remains that modern research on emotion has, in practice, tended to cluster in *universalist* and *anti-universalist* camps – something that has greatly impacted the overall development of knowledge on the topic.

This Cambridge Element surveys and assesses how scholars have variously responded to this debate, by reflecting on the state of knowledge in psychology, neuroscience, sociology, anthropology, philosophy, history, linguistics, and literary/cultural studies. Section 1 presents the universalist case, while Section 2 presents the anti-universalist case; Section 3 considers attempts to reconcile the two sides, and offers some suggestions on how we might move beyond a reductive opposition.

Though I have a wide interest in both emotion and universality, I am by trade a literary scholar – which means, of course, that most of the fields I survey in this Element are not ones in which I am formally trained. I have attempted to provide as fair and accurate an overview as I possibly can – and I have consulted with scholars within the fields I discuss – but the inescapable fact is that I am an outsider to most of the disciplines I cover. So it is certain that, in places, my approach and claims will appear to some degree idiosyncratic to readers more thoroughly anchored in a given field, and I offer this project with full acknowledgment that (say) a neuroscientist or a philosopher might object to some of the specific ways that I characterize their field. My hope is that the overall assessment I present will excuse the local matters that a more specialized reader might quibble with. My approach is generally historical; I have attempted to represent the development of various fields, and for this reason still make mention of evidence and outlooks that have been subsequently abandoned or revised. I have also rarely attempted to critique or problematize the actual research being presented, but rather have focused on reporting the claims made by the authors; although my own outlook peeks out a bit in Section 3, I have generally attempted to be a neutral observer. For matters of space, it is impossible to offer an overview of approaches to emotion or emotion theory; for this, the most comprehensive resource is Scarantino (2024). Finally, it will be noted that my discussion of "what is universality" is deferred until the final section; this is by design, as scholarship has generally proceeded on both sides of the debate without defining this central term.

Despite its short length, it is my hope that this Element will represent the most complete cross-disciplinary treatment of emotional universality to date, and that readers will leave with a clear sense of the scholarly terrain, from which they may make their own assessments of the evidence and judgments on the issue.

# 1 The Universalist Case

In the history of human thought, the capacity for emotion has most regularly been understood to emerge from a universal nature that is (in broad strokes) shared by all members of our species. Although accounts have become increasingly sophisticated, the basic belief that emotions are meaningfully universal has enjoyed remarkable currency in the modern era, and continues to profoundly influence contemporary work on emotion in a number of fields.

## Psychology

For 150 years, a basic belief in the universality of emotion has been a cornerstone of modern psychology; indeed, in a recent survey of current researchers in the field, 88 percent of affective scientists endorsed the statement "there is compelling evidence for universals in any aspect of emotion" (Ekman, 2016, p. 32). However, this statement belies the fierce theoretical disagreements about emotion that occur in psychology, and the devil is in the details. While most psychologists probably agree that the fundamental capacity for emotion is a human universal, there have been intense conflicts regarding more specific issues, most notably whether individual emotions themselves universally occur in human populations. Those on the pro-side of the debate generally maintain that we can point to a set of specific human emotions that are meaningfully universal – that is, they consistently produce observable manifestations – which are thought to have developed as adaptive responses to frequently reoccurring selection pressures in the evolutionary history of the species.

This universalist position is most readily advocated by a family of *basic* or *discrete* emotion theories (Shiota, 2024). These theories are anchored in the work of Darwin (1872), who famously examined facial expressions corresponding to discrete emotional states: "I have endeavoured to show in considerable detail," he writes, "that all the chief expressions exhibited by man are the same throughout the world" (p. 361). In the mid twentieth century, Darwin's analysis was influentially revived by Tomkins (1962), who largely inaugurated the modern research tradition on discrete, universal emotions (see also Plutchik, 1962). Tomkins argued that there were nine universal emotions, reflected in *innate affect programs* – subcortical structures that, when activated, reliably trigger a pattern of motivational, behavioral, and physiological responses, including displays of the stereotypical facial patterns investigated by Darwin. Indeed, the presumed universality of emotional facial expression was central to Tomkins's theory, so his students began to seek empirical evidence concerning the cross-cultural facial recognition of emotion (Ekman, 1971; Izard, 1971); these researchers (most notably Ekman) would go on to develop the so-called Basic Emotion Theory (BET), the central theoretical framework that posits the natural existence of a small number of certain categorically discrete, universal human emotions, such as *happiness, fear, anger, sadness, disgust,* and *surprise* (Cordaro, 2024; Ekman, 1992, 1999; Ekman & Cordaro, 2011; Levenson, 1999, 2011; Shiota, 2024).

As we will see further in Section 3, BET has evolved considerably over the past half-century, but advocates generally agree that basic emotions are biologically universal evolutionary adaptations that are "physiologically, neurologically, functionally, and behaviorally distinct from one another" (Cordaro, 2024, p. 5). Historically, much BET research has focused on the facial expression of emotion; decades of cross-cultural analysis has led theorists to conclude that each basic emotion triggers a stereotypical pattern of universal facial movements that can be recognized by people across the world at a much higher rate than chance alone (Elfenbein & Ambady, 2002; Ekman, 1993; Ekman et al., 1987; Izard, 1994; Witkower, Rule, & Tracy, 2023). Evidence suggests that other forms of affective social communication may also be universally recognized, such as bodily expression (Witkower et al., 2021) and nonverbal vocalizations (Juslin & Laukka, 2003; Laukka & Elfenbein, 2021; Sauter et al., 2010, 2015). Basic emotion theorists equally argue that discrete emotions characteristically inspire certain response patterns in the body's autonomic nervous system (ANS); particular basic emotions are thought to generate specific ANS responses that can be to some extent distinguished from one another (Ekman, Levenson, & Friesen, 1983; Kreibig, 2010; Levenson, 1992, 2003; Levenson, Ekman, & Friesen, 1990; Levenson et al., 1992; but see Levenson, 2014 for methodological issues). In general, most BET theorists have historically maintained that the central emotions of human life have some sort of discrete, observable universal *signatures* that are biologically grounded in the body.

As mentioned, basic and discrete theories of emotion maintain that particular emotions are universal biological adaptations, so evolutionary psychology (Buss, 2015; Cosmides & Tooby, 2013; Tooby, 2020) provides complementary evidence for the universality of emotion. (Though, to be clear, many nonuniversalist theories of emotion equally ground their models in evolutionary theory, so it is important not to simply conflate an evolutionary approach with a universalist, discrete emotion approach.) Put simply, researchers working in this mode view emotions as universal adaptations of our species' mental architecture, which emerged in the long course of mammalian development as responses to increase fitness in light of certain ubiquitous situations (Cosmides & Tooby, 2000; Keltner, Haidt, & Shiota, 2006; Nesse, 1990; Nesse & Ellsworth, 2009; Plutchik, 2001, 2003; Tooby & Cosmides, 1990a, 2008, 2015; Tracy, 2014; see also J. H. Turner, 1996, 2021). Many evolutionary approaches to emotion (and psychology more broadly) locate discrete emotions within human nature – that is, "the evolved, reliably developing, species-typical computational and neural architecture of the human mind and brain" (Cosmides & Tooby, 2000, p. 91; see Tooby & Cosmides, 1990b) – and thus universality consequently follows, as further suggested by studies that analyze analogous emotion-like expression in our evolutionary ancestors (Kret et al., 2020; Parr et al., 2007; Vick et al., 2007). A number of discrete emotions have been analyzed in terms of their universal adaptive functions, such as fear (LeDoux, 2012); jealousy (Buss, 2018), anger (Sell, Tooby, & Cosmides, 2009), pride (Cheng, Tracy, & Henrich, 2010), and compassion (Goetz, Keltner, & Simon-Thomas, 2010).

Beyond evolutionary psychology, some researchers in the field of cross-cultural psychology aim to detect not only variants in mental functioning across different populations but also points of regularity and consistency (Keith, 2019; Sinha, 2002). This work has contributed to the development of basic emotion theories by conducting research pointing to the broad universality of emotion in different cultural contexts, most notably in the realm of facial expression and recognition (Hwang & Matsumoto, 2015, 2020; Manokara et al., 2021; Matsumoto, 1990, 1992; Matsumoto & Ekman, 1989; Matsumoto & Willingham, 2006).

Other psychological approaches to emotion complement BET's findings on universality; indeed, some influential scholars like Izard (1977, 1991, 2007, 2009, 2011) do not consider themselves BET theorists per se, but still advocate for discrete, universal emotions. Finally, it must be noted that basic and discrete emotion theories are not the only psychological models of emotion that consider the existence of particular universal emotions. We may also look, for instance, at the category of appraisal theories. Appraisal theory generally maintains that emotions emerge from a computational cognitive process in which humans subjectively evaluate the meaning of stimuli they encounter via a series of categorical criteria (Ellsworth, 2024); along with basic/discrete theories, it is one of the four primary theoretical models of emotion in the contemporary affective sciences. (We will encounter the final two, *psychological construction* and *social construction*, in the next section.) While appraisal theory, broadly speaking, is thus an intellectual competitor of BET, certain models nonetheless posit a similarly universal approach to particular emotions: Moors calls these "flavor 1" (2014, p. 304) or "biological" (2022, p. 175) appraisal theories. These models, she writes, split emotional episodes "into a limited number of subsets, corresponding to the specific emotions figuring in natural language (e.g. anger, fear, sadness)," and are thus "compatible with affect program theories" (2014, pp. 303, 304). Appraisal theories that might be thought to fall under this umbrella include Arnold (1960), Lazarus (1991), Oatley & Johnson-Laird (2011), and Roseman (1984, 2011, 2013).

## Neuroscience

Affective neuroscience seeks to elucidate how emotions function at the neural level (Aromy & Vuilleumier, 2013). For many researchers, a fundamental premise is that the human emotional brain evolved from earlier animal brain systems – with "partly separate neural circuits for different emotion related responses [including] autonomic output, freezing, fixed action patterns, and unconditioned approach or withdrawal" (Rolls, 2017, p. 252) – and thus much work on human emotionality is anchored in a universalist perspective, which maintains that "emotions are ubiquitous across species and evolved by natural selection" (Adolphs & Anderson, 2018, p. 308; see also Adolphs, 2017).

In the 1990s, a number of pioneering neuroscientists began to study the basic neural components of emotion systems, finding structures in the brain that give rise to affective feelings in humans (Johnston & Olson, 2015). "At least for some emotions," Ledoux argued, "the evidence for an innate, biological organization is quite strong" (1996, p. 121); he famously reconstructed the neural pathways of fear responses in the rodent brain, which pointed to human functioning (see also Ledoux, 2000). In his study of patients with brain injury, Damasio argued that the limbic system (particularly the amygdala) was vital to the operation of "primary" emotions, which he describes as "innate [and] preorganized" (1994, p. 133; see also Damasio 1995, 1999, 2003); for him, emotions form a category of *action programmes*, or "sets of innate, programmed physiological actions aimed at addressing the detected [neural] changes and thereby maintaining or restoring homeostatic balance" (Damasio & Carvalho, 2013, p. 144). Though disagreeing with Damasio's emphasis on the role of bodily feedback on emotional experience, Rolls (1999) similarly examined the "neural bases of emotion," taking a primarily evolutionary perspective; he argued specifically that "developments in primates in the structure and connection of neural systems involved in emotion such as the amygdala and orbitofrontal cortex [are] particularly important for understanding emotion in humans" (p. 75). Somewhat differently, Panksepp (1998, 2005, 2011, 2012; Montag & Panksepp, 2016; Panksepp & Bivven, 2012; see also Montag & David, 2020) identified the basic emotional circuits of mammalian brains, arguing that we can detect neural mechanisms for affective systems related to SEEKING, RAGE, FEAR, LUST, CARE, PANIC, and PLAY; these "underlying circuits for primary-process emotions were evolutionarily programmed/prewired" (Panksepp & Watt, 2011, p. 390). This work, like that of Lane, Reiman, Ahern, Schwartz, and Davidson (1997), assumes that neural correlates for basic emotional functioning can be discovered.

In human subjects, this first wave of affective neuroscience relied on things like lesion, electrical stimulation, and imaging studies to analyze the neural underpinnings of emotions; researchers generally attempted to associate particular areas of the brain with particular discrete emotions. Two early meta-analyses found at least partial support of basic emotion theory; Phan, Wager, Taylor, and Liberzon (2002) associated particular individual emotions with specific locations within the brain, while Murphy, Nimmo-Smith, and Lawrence (2003) identified "considerable support ... for the affect program accounts of emotion," noting that while emotions may not be "represented by entirely distinct neural circuits, it seems reasonable to conclude that the underlying neural systems are separate in part" (p. 227). The meta-analysis of Vytal and Hamann (2010) offered stronger evidence: not only "each of the basic emotion states examined (anger, fear, sadness, anger, and disgust) was consistently associated across studies with characteristic patterns of region brain activity" but also "each basic emotion was reliably distinguished or differentiated from the other emotions on the basis of its characteristic pattern of brain activation" (p. 2879).

This emphasis on patterns is crucial, because when subsequent experiments failed to show a one-to-one correspondence between brain regions and discrete emotions – for example, when the amygdala turned out not to be the simple "fear center" of the brain – researchers in the last decade or so began to use more sophisticated methods of imaging (such as multivariate pattern classification) to record the broad patterns of cross-region neural activity that seem to correspond to individual emotions (Kragel & LaBar, 2013, 2014). Such studies seemed to find "mappings between neural activation patterns and categorically distinct emotional experiences" (Kragel & LaBar, 2015, p. 1447) and suggest that "information encoded in both neural ensembles and whole-brain activation patterns can be utilized to predict affective dimensions and discrete emotions with high levels of specificity" (Kragel & LaBar, 2016, p. 453). For example, Saarimäki et al. (2016) used multivariate analysis to show that "all 6 basic emotions have distinguishable but spatially distributed neural signatures in the human brain," signatures that "generalize across different emotion-eliciting conditions and also across individuals" (p. 2564). Such experimental results suggest that "different emotions are represented in the brain in a distinguishable manner, yet in partly overlapping regions" (Saarimäki et al., 2018, p. 477). Accordingly, current thinking suggests that the "discreteness" of basic emotions is "best understood as widespread, system-level patterned activity, rather than selective regional or systemic engagement during specific emotions" (Nummenmaa & Saarimäki, 2019, p. 7), and the most recent work looks for whole-brain *functional* (as opposed to *physical*) connectivity patterns in the experience of basic emotions (Saarimäki et al., 2022).

## Sociology

"Traditionally," it was said not long ago, "emotion is a topic more central to psychology than to sociology" – but foundational sociologists like Marx, Weber, and Durkheim gave considerable attention to the operation of affective forces, and since the 1970s the sociology of emotion has truly emerged as a dedicated subfield of research (Smith-Lovin & Winkielman, 2010, p. 327; for overviews see; Ariza, 2021; Bericat, 2016; Lively, 2024; Stets, 2010; Stets, 2012; Stets & Turner, 2006, 2008, 2014; Turner & Stets, 2005). In many ways, debates about emotion in sociology ran parallel with those we have already explored in psychology (Smith-Lovin & Winkielman, 2010). Almost immediately, sociologists began to question whether emotions should be understood as biologically based, quasi-universal phenomena – the *positivist, naturalizing*, or *organismic* view – or whether they were more meaningfully shaped by social and cultural forces – the *constructionist* view, which we will see more of in Section 2 (Hochschild, 1983a; Kemper, 1981). In an early contribution to the field, Kemper (1981) neatly delineated some initial terms of this opposition; in terms of universality, the positivists most vitally emphasized "the importance of the biological and physiological substrate in the determination of specific emotions" (p. 336). Consistent with other fields, in the most basic sense these contrasting viewpoints continue to account for "the two main trends of sociology of emotions up to the present day" (Longo, 2020, p. 42).

Those outside the discipline may be initially surprised to find the enthusiasm for the universalist outlook, but this in part reflects the larger legacy of much early sociology, which often "looked for what is generic and universal in human behaviors and patterns of socio organization" (J. H. Turner, 2021, p. 4). Given sociology's historical interest in making "systematic and universalistic" claims about "the nature of man and society," it thus makes sense that much work in the field has maintained "that there is a common human nature [and] that emotions, sentiments, feelings, and passions do not vary over time" – it is "only their representation, the forms of their expression, and their philosophical or doctrinal rationalization" that are contextually dependent (Romania, 2022, pp. 106, 107–108). The universalist position of sociology is founded on the same general premises as basic/discrete theories in psychology – that a small set of "primary" emotions are an evolutionarily shaped, biological constant of human nature – and researchers in this mode argue that "a complete theory of emotion must ultimately deal with the fact that emotion is biologically rooted . . . regardless of the degree of social conversion, construction, or management" (Kemper, 1990, p. 21). Turner and Stets (2005), for example, begin their sociology of emotion by announcing that "although there are cultural differences in how emotions are expressed and interpreted, it is now clear that some emotions are universal [and] generated from evolved body systems"; "most scholars would agree," they suggest, that certain basic emotions are "primary or biologically based," and we can thus safely "conclude that happiness, fear, anger, and sadness are universal among humans, with a few other emotions as potential candidates for inclusion in the list of primary emotions" (pp. 11, 13). For such positivist scholars, there is accordingly "nothing antisociological in finding that physiology plays a differentiating and crucial role in the emotions," and this opinion is to a degree common: even sociologists who recommend skepticism toward the "lure" of the neurosciences acknowledge that, in general, constructivist work has "not managed to upset a naturalizing view of emotion" in sociological thought (Kemper, 1981, p. 342; Kleres, 2009, pp. 14, 13). Even beyond basic affective sentiments, we can find a universalizing orientation toward more socially elaborated emotion; consider, for example, Jacobsen's (2019) recent collection *Emotions, Everyday Life and Sociology*, a volume whose chapters on discrete emotions make statements like "courage is universally valued" (Marvasti, 2019, p. 71), "embarrassment as an emotional experience is universal" (Jacobsen & Kristiansen, 2019, p. 105), and "envy is a universal social problem" (Clanton, 2019, p. 150).

But aside from the issue of biological rootedness, sociologists often show universalizing sympathies in their accounts of how emotions function socially – indeed, the very search for "a general sociological theory of emotion" implies the possibility of universal principles of process and function (J. H. Turner, 1999, p. 134), and universalism thus underpins the work of those who believe "the task of the sociology of emotions [most rightly concerns] the interconnection between social structure . . . and certain physiologically specific emotions" (Longo, 2020, p. 42). J. H. Turner (2002), for example, in his theory of interpersonal behavior argues that "transactional needs drive the flow of interaction in certain universal directions, despite the widely varying contexts of encounters" (p. 28); emotions play a central role in how these encounters unfold, and they are thus thought to have universal functions that align with their biological universality. Another example is Barbalet (1998), who argues that "emotion terms can be developed in and applied to the analysis of social structure": thus "rationality, class structure, social action, social conformity, basic rights, and social change [can be] considered through discussion of a particular emotion or set of emotions which both characteristically pertains to each of them and elucidates the processes to which each is subject" (p. 1). Perhaps most notably, Kemper (1978, 1987, 1990, 2006; Kemper & Collins, 1990) very much honors the physiological grounding of basic emotions, but argues that they are made salient in social encounters through linkage to the two central dimensions of personal interaction: *power* and *status*. Most importantly for our current purposes, a "fundamental assumption" of his theory is that "the power-status antecedents of specific emotions apply universally across the spectrum of social and demographic categories" – because "were the primary emotions to vary in their relational precursors, considerable social ambiguity would result," a fact that fundamentally problematizes how "emotion might, in an evolutionary sense applying to all humans, have emerged" (2006, pp. 109–110). Thamm (2004), building on this work, finds that "the *structure* of human groups and emotions are universal," and that "there is a direct link between specific universal social substructures and specific universal emotions" (pp. 189–190).

## Anthropology

"Affect has never been a focus of anthropological research," Epstein (1992, p. 2) wrote some time ago, and Stodulka (2017, p. 12) more recently observed that "emotions are rarely a primary theoretical focus of ethnographies and predominantly remain implicit subject matter"; this is reflected, for example, by the fact that there is no section devoted to emotion in the 102 chapters of *21st Century Anthropology: A Reference Handbook* (Birx, 2010). In anthropology, emotions have, to some degree, been undertheorized in the broader sense, with the focus usually fixed on giving accounts of what they *do* in a given society (Beatty, 2014).

But this does not mean that anthropologists have remained quiet about the subject. Researchers increasingly acknowledge that emotions crucially shape the anthropologist's experiences in the field (Behar, 1996; Davies & Spencer, 2010; Lo Bosco, 2021; Spencer & Davies, 2010; Stodulka, Selim, & Mattes, 2018; Stodulka, Dinkelaker, & Thajib, 2019), and beyond this, there has more generally been foundational work on anthropological emotion in the last 50 years.

(It is important to recognize, though, that the heyday of modern anthropological research on emotion was in the last decades of the last century: noting in 2013 the "apparent thinness of current emotion research," Beatty observed that "an overview of highlights in the anthropology of emotion would show that the major contributions have mostly been made some time ago" [p. 415].) Anthropological accounts of emotion have shown both explicit and implicit interest in the issue of affective universality – perhaps unsurprisingly, given that human universality is a larger concern of anthropology, in the sense that the discipline has historically been at least partly concerned with "the study of human nature in light of human variation" (Shore, 2000, p. 81; see Roughley, 2000). In terms of emotion, the field has seen a division between universalist and constructivist positions that broadly reflects what we have seen elsewhere (Leavitt, 1996; Svašek, 2005).

Although much anthropology of emotion has taken a constructivist approach, there is a core universalist sympathy that runs through the history of the discipline. Following Boas (1910), modern anthropology was historically premised on the so-called psychic unity of mankind, the notion that there is "an essential similarity of mental endowment" in all peoples, and that "diverse [cross-cultural] phenomena are based on similar psychic processes" (pp. 372, 384; see Shore, 1996; Beatty, 2019). But, as we will consider in the next section, commitment to this position does not mean that the discipline became fundamentally invested in enumerating transcultural human universals: Boas's students primarily utilized our species' common psychic potentiality to establish a cultural relativism that investigated the unique features of different population groups, and this tendency has endured in some of the most important subsequent anthropological works on emotion, especially (we will see) works that developed cultural relativism into a genuine constructivist position.

Despite this, however, there have always been anthropologists who adopted a universalist approach to the basic question of emotion. H. Geertz (1959), for example, in her study of Javanese socialization processes, argues that "the range and quality of emotional experience is potentially the same for all human beings"; concepts like "anxiety and hostility, insofar as they are operationally defined in terms of scientific theory, refer to basically human – that is, universal – emotions" (p. 225). In his analysis of symbols, V. Turner (1967) similarly refers to "referents of a grossly physiological character, relating to general human experience of an emotional kind" (p. 54). Though Myers (1979) acknowledged that "socialization selects, elaborates, and emphasizes certain qualitative aspects of emotion," his treatment of Pintupi affective vocabulary explicitly affirmed H. Geertz's earlier position (353).

The 1980s saw the most concentrated and explicit expansion of the construct-ivist position in anthropology, but affective universalism still endured among some scholars. In a famous review of C. Geertz (1980), Leach (1981) took aim at the entire field designated "cultural anthropology" – exclaiming that "I can make no sense of a line of thought which claims that 'passions' are culturally defined," and denounced that assumption "that human individuals are products of their culture rather than of their genetic predisposition" (p. 32). Shweder and Levine's (1984) *Culture Theory: Essays on Mind, Self, and Emotion* – a classic collection on the anthropology of emotion – contains several essays that support emotional universality; Spiro (1984), for example, suggests that "human feel-ings and the ways in which they work are determined not so much by the characteristics of particularistic culture patterns but by the transcultural charac-teristics of a generic human mind" (p. 334), while Levy (1984) argues that "there is no reason to think that some *dimensions* of the emotional feeling do not vary cross-culturally" and that "the central tendencies named by various emo-tional terms are probably universal" (pp. 223, 229). R. Rosaldo (1984), in the same year, published a celebrated, autobiographical essay that chronicled how he came to understand the Illongot practice of headhunting only after the tragic death of his wife, a fellow anthropologist; though not a strict universalist, there is some degree of regularity implied in the statement that his own parallel "personal experience" enabled him to "apprehend the force of emotions in another culture" (p. 188).

Some anthropologists continued to anchor their subsequent work in biology, against the fashion of the day; Gerber (1985), for instance, assumes that "emotions arise at least in part from a biological substrate ... which limits the range of emotional variation across cultures" (p. 121), while Epstein (1992), drawing on Tomkins and Ekman, laments that "cultural analysis ignores bio-logical factors" (p. 11). Lyon (1995), going further, argues that "the cultural constructionist approach to emotion has real limitations," because "emotion is more than a domain of cultural conception, more than mere construction, and thus cannot be treated merely as parallel to constructions such as self and person" (p. 247): It is vital, she argues, to honor the role of the biological body in emotional experience. And more generally, the broad importance of cross-cultural universals in anthropology was buttressed by the work of Brown (1991, 2000, 2001); facial expressions of emotions (among many other things) are considered in his analysis to be meaningfully universal.

Finally, the presumed universalism of emotion has played a specific methodo-logical role in the theorization of anthropological fieldwork. I refer to the work-ings of empathy, because it has historically been thought that a framework of shared universal experience allows researchers to empathetically comprehend cultures that are drastically different from their own (Leavitt, 1996). While constructivists have attacked this position as ethnocentric, it still has currency; Lindholm, for example, suggests that the "whole disciplinary practice [of anthropology] is based on feelings of empathy" (2007, p. 31).

## Philosophy

The philosophy of emotion is a robust research field (for overviews, see Brady, 2024; Campeggiani, 2023; Cohen & Stern, 2017; Deigh, 2013; Deonna & Teroni, 2012; Goldie, 2010; Griffiths, 2017; Moors, 2022; Scarantino, 2016; Scarantino & de Sousa, 2018; Solomon, 2004; Tappolet, 2023). But compared to those in other disciplines, philosophers have devoted somewhat less attention to explicitly arguing for or against the universality of emotion. In 2002, Solomon – one of the most prominent philosophers of emotion in the last half-century – remarked that philosophers instead "tend to argue over whether an emotion is a feeling or a set of beliefs or judgments or evaluations . . . [so the questions] of whether the feelings of emotion are learned or innate and how they are based on physiological if not also neurological processes hardly get raised" (pp. 119–120). More recently, Tappolet (2023) observes that most philosophers of emotion are centrally concerned with "develop[ing] a theory that aims at spelling out what emotions consist in, so as to be able to distinguish emotions from other states" (pp. 11–12) – so although they have shown a robust interest in the multitude of ways that emotions might be considered, the universality question per se has not been the subject of the same rigorous debate that has been found in other fields. What has been fiercely debated is the related question of whether or not emotions are a *natural kind* (Charland, 2001, 2002; Cochraine, 2019; De Sousa, 1987; Griffiths, 1997, 2001, 2004a, 2004b; Prinz, 2004; Rorty, 1980; Scarantino, 2009, 2012a, 2012b; Taylor, 2020) – that is, whether they form a class of entities about which scientific generalizations can be made. Many philosophers, Solomon (1995) noted earlier, seem to work with the assumption that "there is *some* natural repertoire of emotions that constitutes 'human nature,' some set of 'basic' emotions" (p. 258) – a fundamentally universalist premise – but there is disagreement about whether *all* emotions are universal, or whether all things that get called *emotion* belong to the same scientifically valid category.

But despite this, Goldie (2002) observes that there is a long philosophical tradition of believing that a certain small set of "basic emotions [are] common to all humans": it is present in the work of the Stoics, Descartes, Spinoza, and Hobbes, to name just a few (p. 87). As Griffiths (2017) notes, more contemporary work on the emotions is commonly "pursued by adherents of philosophical naturalism" – that is, "the view that philosophy deals in knowledge of the natural world no different in principle from that revealed by the sciences" (p. 107); Brady (2024) suggests that this "naturalistic or empirically based philosophy ... takes its lead from empirical science, seeking to make theoretical sense of empirical data [and thus] closely resembles psychological theorizing" (p. 216). This work tends to show a preference for the basic emotion paradigm in the mode of Tomkins and Ekman; this is perhaps because, Tappolet (2023) argues, basic emotion theory can be seen as generally compatible with what have been identified as the primary philosophical approaches to emotion (motivation theories, evaluation theories, and feeling theories; see Scarantino, 2016; Scarantino & de Sousa, 2018).

In this sense, many philosophers align themselves (to some degree) with what might be thought of as universalist psychological theories of emotion. Charland (1995), for instance, approvingly cites Ekman (and other empirical researchers) to conclude that "affect is an independent perceptual system that exhibits significant modular factors" (p. 295). Griffiths (1997) does not believe that the category of *emotion* is a natural kind, but he still acknowledges the existence of certain discrete affect programs, and argues that "the imperialist claims of social constructionists to explain the whole domain of emotional phenomena are unjustified" (p. 9). Like Griffiths, Goldie (2002) endorses the notion of *affect program responses* (pp. 105–106). DeLancey (2002) grounds his philosophy of mind and artificial intelligence in the workings of affect programs and basic emotion theory; what's more, he explicitly sets out to "confront social construc-tionism," arguing that "it is not ... a viable alternative to the affect program theory or any other naturalistic theory of the emotions" (p. 70). Also anchoring his work in affect programs, Prinz (2004) argues that "basic emotions are innate emotions that are not derived from other emotions" (p. 88); in his theory, all emotions are embodied appraisals, with basic emotions giving rise to complex emotions (via blending or cognitive elaboration). Clark (2010) argues for basic emotions, and believes that they and higher cognitive emotions "have deep roots in our biology" (p. 90). Finally, Cochraine (2019) emphasizes "type-specific response patterns" of emotion (p. 86), and takes a dimensional approach to argue that certain "basic features of [emotions] are culturally universal" (p. 209). The universalist premise of basic emotion theory, then, has been productively used in philosophical work.

## History

In past centuries, historians routinely adopted a universalist approach to emo-tion, considering affectivity in terms of an unchanging human nature (see

Boddice, 2024; Reddy, 2009). There is, however, no meaningful contemporary strand of historical research that is anchored in a universal approach to emotion: as we will see in the next section, history is perhaps the most unified discipline when it comes to the universalism/constructivism division, and opposition to universality has been said to be a foundational premise of the historical study of emotion.

## Linguistics

Psychologists have shown regular attention to the connection between emotion and language (see Gallois et al., 2021), but this relationship is of particular concern to those working in the language sciences. This is with good reason: "all speaking and writing," Wilce (2009) notes, is "inherently emotional to a greater or lesser extent," in the sense that "nearly every dimension of every language at least potentially encodes emotion" (p. 3; see also Pritzker, Fenigsen, & Wilce, 2020; Schiewer, Altarriba, & Ng, 2022–2023). Similar to what we've seen in other fields, in linguistics, a "debate has been raging between researchers who defend a more universalist perspective on emotions and others who feel that emotions should be investigated using a more relativist perspective, with a focus on the differences across languages and cultures" (Dewaele, 2010, pp. 17–18). The universalist perspective on emotion emerges from a larger disciplinary investment in universality: since the second half of the twentieth century, Bickel (2014) observes, "linguistics has sent a strong message that despite all diversity, languages are built on a single universal grammar" (p. 102), and "a long-standing and dominant view" has maintained that "language is the product of an innate, universal, domain-specific and encapsulated module" (Majid, 2012, p. 432; see, for example, Degli Esposti, Altmann, & Pachet, 2016; Greenberg, 1975). Indeed, the concept of universality has long been central to modern linguistics, and researchers have variously found patterns of universality in natural language components such as *semantics, connotative or affective meaning, phonology, grammar*, and *lexicon*, among others (Hupka, Lenton, & Hutchison, 1999, p. 247).

Studies on the linguistic universality of emotion have generally attempted to demonstrate patterns of cross-cultural regularity in the semantic and categorical meanings of emotion words. Some representative examples can give a sense of this research. Earlier work by Herrmann and Raybeck (1981), for example, used multidimensional scaling to investigate the meaning of emotion concepts across six cultures; they found "cross-cultural agreement [was] quite high" (p. 194). Romney, Moore, and Rusch (1997) found that "English-speaking and Japanese-speaking subjects share a single model of the semantic structure of emotion terms"; culture-specific models based on English and Japanese norms "account[ed] for relatively little of the total variance" (p. 5489). Church, Katigbak, Reyes, and Jensen (1998) compared the lexical and conceptual organization of emotion terms in English and Filipino, finding "better support for the cross-cultural comparability of emotion concepts and experience than for a strong social constructivist view" (p. 63). Moore, Romney, Hsia, and Rusch (1999) similarly found that "Chinese-, English-, and Japanese-speaking subjects assign basically similar meanings to 15 common emotion terms"; they argue that "the differences among the languages are genuine and statistically significant but small," meaning that the findings are "consistent with previous research traditions that posit cultural and semantic universals" (p. 529). In his "semantic description of emotion predicates in Amharic," Amberber (2001) begins by "assum[ing] a distinct cognitive domain which specialises in the emotions, and that the basic architecture of this cognitive domain is innate and universal" (p. 35); within this framework, his study "shows that emotional universals are borne out by the Amharic data" (p. 65). In a wider study, Hupka, Lenton, and Hutchinson (1999) found remarkable consistencies in the labeling of emotion categories across a survey of the world's languages; these findings, they conclude, "strongly suggest that the lexical regularity, if not based on social and phenomenological experiences common to the human species, surely is founded on innate principles of human language" (p. 260). And in the twenty-first century, scholars from several disciplines created a psycholinguistic instrument (called "GRID") to compare the cross-cultural meaning of emotion words (Fontaine, Scherer, & Soriano, 2013); researchers using this tool have found "evidence for substantial convergence of emotion concepts across cultures," leading to the conclusion that "cognitive representations of lexical meaning (i.e. semantic concepts) of emotions such as joy, anger, or sadness are remarkably similar within and across languages and cultures" (Loderer et al., 2020, pp. 1483, 1480).

Beyond semantic meaning, researchers have looked for cross-cultural consistency in other domains. For example, a valence analysis of millions of words in 10 languages led Dodds et al. (2015) to conclude that "human language present[s] an emotional spectrum with a universal, self-similar positive bias" in usage frequency (p. 2394). This work extends even to the sounds of words: Auracher, Albers, Zhai, Gareeva, and Stavniychuk (2010) found that "participants tend to use similar consonants independent of the mother tongue to encode specific emotional states" (p. 3) – cross-linguistically, nasal (*m*, *n*) sounds are linked to sad feelings, while plosive (*p*, *b*, *t*, and *d*) sounds are linked to happy feelings – while most recently, Shakuf et al. (2022) have shown evidence for emotional universality in prosody (i.e., the rhythm, stress, and intonation of speech), meaning that speakers can accurately assess certain kinds of emotional content (such as anger, fear, happiness, and sadness) even in languages they do not understand.

Finally, metaphors hold particular importance to the language of emotion, as research suggests that their usage is "especially frequent when the topic is emotion, and their frequency increases with emotional intensity" (Crawford, 2009, p. 130; see Ortony & Fainsilber, 1989). Matsunaka, Chen, and Shinohara (2023), in fact, note that "the issue of universality and cross-linguistic variability of emotion metaphors is one of the most controversial topics in cognitive linguistics" (n.p.). From a universalist perspective, cognitive linguists in the conceptual metaphor theory tradition (Lakoff & Johnson, 1980) argue that certain *primary metaphors* reflect simple experiential patterns that "map fundamental perceptual concepts onto equally fundamental but not directly perceptual ones"; because "humans everywhere share the basic patterns of perception and experience that are reflected in primary metaphors, these patterns ought to show up in languages around the world," and many primary metaphors (such as BIG IS IMPORTANT) are in fact "widespread across languages that are not related genetically, areally, or culturally" (Grady, 2007, pp. 192, 194; see also Grady, 1997).

In terms of emotion, linguists have influentially argued that "systems of emotion metaphors arise from the physiology of emotions" (Lakoff, 2014, p. 4). Lakoff (1987) draws on the work of Ekman to suggest that basic human emotions are "basic-level concepts [with] basic-level primary, and centrality" that manifest in embodied metaphors reflecting physiology (p. 14). In the classic example, the fact that the experience of anger entails both the increase of skin temperature and blood pressure and the decrease of visual perception and fine motor control is said to lead to the cross-language ubiquity of metaphors such as *boiling mad, he exploded, blind with rage*, etc. (Lakoff, 2014, p. 4; see Lakoff & Kövecses, 1987; Wilkowski et al., 2009). Emanatian (1995), for example, suggests that "the two semantic domains of *eating* and *heat* may be favored cross-culturally as vehicles for conceptualizing lust and sex" (p. 164), while Crawford (2009) reviews empirical evidence for the ubiquity of concepts such as *GOOD as UP, GOOD is HIGH in Pitch, GOOD is BIG (or MORE), GOOD is BRIGHT*, and *GOOD is GETTING CLOSER*, concluding that "abstract concepts [like emotion] are conceptualized in terms of more concrete, embodied physical domains" (p. 138).

## Literary and Cultural Studies

Although emotion has long been understood as central to the analysis and appreciation of literature, there has not been a tremendous amount of modern scholarship that specifically addresses the universality of emotion. To some extent, it was simply assumed for centuries that the mark of a great book was its ability to universally appeal to readers, usually at an emotional level (see Long, 1909). In the last 50 years, however, there has been a dramatic shift in how literary critics think about universality; as we will see in the next section, it is a taboo concept for the majority of twenty-first-century literary theorists, most of whom find the idea of universality to be (at best) naïve and (more regularly) a politically retrograde tool of ideological oppression.

While universality has largely fallen out of fashion in English departments, there are some theorists who have attempted to revive an approach to literary criticism based on the assumption of a common human nature; the "literary humanism" of Mousley (2007, 2011) is one such example, which (in terms of emotion) notes that one "problem with anti-universalism is that it has discredited the language of human feeling and engagement which we might want to use to describe the experience of literature" (2007, p. 8). Human nature is even more central to scholars working in the subfield of evolutionary literary theory (J. Carroll, 2018; J. Carroll, Clasen, & Jonsson, 2020; Jonsson, 2020, 2021), which sometimes touches upon emotion; J. Carroll (2022a), for example, "uses an evolutionary model of human nature to organize emotion terms within eight categories, [which] serve as the framework for understanding emotions in individuals (authors, characters, and readers), literary genres, and literary periods" (p. 86).

But there are other scholars who more specifically devote themselves to analyzing the universality of emotion; among these, P. Hogan (2003, 2008a, 2008b, 2011a, 2011b, 2013, 2018, 2022) is by far the most prominent and influential. Having studied an enormous range of works from unrelated, precolonial literary traditions, Hogan first argues for the existence of literary universals, primarily realized in cross-cultural patterns of recurrence in various elements of literature. But even more importantly, his expertise in affective science causes him to posit that "the universality of human emotion systems (such as attachment and fear) provide the groundwork for an explanation of story universals": that is, "different emotion systems define different types of goals," and "on the basis of the cross-cultural research ... we can isolate and describe universal story patterns in terms of agents pursuing goals, goals that are themselves a function of our specific emotion systems" (2022, p. 335). Hogan thus sees the universality of emotion as central to the operation of literature more broadly, and he has traced the intersection of literary and emotional universals across many groundbreaking books and articles. (The connection between basic literary forms and basic emotional experiences was also explored by a variety of ancient theorists, such as Aristotle and those in the Indian *rasa* tradition; see N. Carroll, 2022; L. P. Hogan, 2011.)

Besides Hogan, a handful of other literary critics have similarly adopted a universalist perspective. We encountered above Oatley's general theory of discrete emotion, but he (a fiction writer himself) has also developed a foundational body of research pertaining to literature and emotion (2006, 2011, 2012, 2016); most recently, he has developed a structural account of how poetry evokes emotion, arguing that poems prompt various mental simulations that generate "basic emotions [like] happiness, sadness, anger, and anxiety" (Johnson-Laird & Oatley, 2022, p. 1). Oatley is a cognitive theorist, and those in the broader subfield of cognitive literary studies sometimes equally touch upon emotion from an implicitly universalist position (see Zunshine, 2015). More specifically, literary theorists interested in embodied cognition and simulation – particularly the effect of the mirror neuron network – often take an universalist perspective; Wojciehowski and Gallese (2022), pioneers of this approach, argue that "the activity of reading fictional narratives activates the same neural circuits that we use in everyday life – circuits that underpin all of our own actions, emotional and sensory experiences" (p. 62; see also Gallese & Wojciehowski, 2018; Wojciehowski & Gallese, 2011).

In recent years, literary scholars have continued to intermittently ground their work using a universalist approach to emotion, either indirectly or directly. Asher (2017), for example, focuses on the ethical implications of literary emotions, but speaks in passing of "universal emotional patterns" and "universal emotional currents" (pp. 159, 163). Extending the work of Hogan, Singh (2021) suggests that "a universal narrative structure (the sympathetic plot) recurs because it induces pleasure" (p. 186). Zeng (2022) argues that "universality in literature means that a piece of literary work is able to reflect universal emotions," applying this standard to advocate for the emotional universality of Emily Brontë's poem "Remembrance" (p. 313). And my own work of literary criticism (Irish, 2018, 2020, 2023) often adopts the premise that certain prototypical features of emotion are functionally universal, even if the specific ways that emotions manifest are shaped by cultural and historical circumstances.

Beyond literary studies, work on the dynamics of art more generally will often adopt a universalist perspective, as in the attempt of Menninghaus et al. (2019), to define the structural features of aesthetic emotions. Furthermore, the literary treatment of emotion complexly overlaps with so-called Affect Theory – a branch of poststructuralist cultural theory that is, in practice, often developed and employed by literary scholars (see Ahern, 2024; Gregg & Seigworth, 2010). Affect theorists sometimes engage universalist emotion paradigms – Sedgwick and Frank (1995), for example, were famously influenced by Tomkins – and their emphasis on the human body is meant as a corrective to their critical tradition's hyperfocus on language. Nonetheless, the poststructuralist foundation of their work fundamentally ensures that they are not biologically determinist in a way that would be familiar to universalist scientists – and it is also generally the case that their interaction with affective science is superficial and idiosyncratic, as individual experiments and theories are used as a platform for philosophical musings, rather than as a source of empirical data (see Hogan, 2018).

## 2 The Anti-universalist Case

Although much thinking about emotion, we saw in the last section, is premised on the basic universality of human emotional experience, this is not the only way to consider the matter: there also exists a robust intellectual tradition, developed especially across the last half-century, which sees emotions as fundamentally *constructed* by various social and psychological forces. Rather than emphasizing the presumed universality of emotion, scholars working in this mode generally prioritize the extent to which emotions are shaped by cultural, temporal, and psychological conditions.

## Psychology

While the modern constructivist tradition in psychology is usually said to start with the work of James (1884, 1890), historical accounts of anti-universalism often point to the landmark study of Schachter and Singer (1962), which suggested that people will apply different emotional labels to the same physiological experience depending on the context in which that experience occurs. In response to the rise of BET, more psychologists in subsequent decades would tend to the contextual features of emotion, most notably in the development of *social constructivist* approaches (see Mesquita & Parkinson, 2024; Oatley, 1993). Reflecting (as we will see) a broader trend in the social sciences, constructivist psychologist denied that a basic set of emotions are cross-cultural universal, stressing instead that affective experience is primarily shaped by the specific social parameters of an individual's developmental and cultural context; most notable is the work of Averill (1980, 1994, 2012), whose approach privileges not "a biological level of analysis," but rather sees emotions as "socially constituted syndromes, the meaning and function of which are determined primarily by the social system(s) of which they are a part" (1982, p. 19; see also Ratner, 1989). Others questioned the categorical validity of the BET model, arguing that there is little evidence to suggest that a small set of English-specific emotion terms accurately reflects a universal quality of affective experience, and that such a method of classification is not actually scientifically valuable (Ortony & Turner, 1990; Russell, 1991; see also Ortony, 2022). Indeed, the categorical tendency of BET was explicitly challenged by the fresh development of *dimensional* models of affect, which assessed emotions not in terms of individuated universal signatures, but rather saw them as characterized by descriptive dimensional features such as degree of *valence* and degree of *arousal*; rather than positing sharply discrete emotions, such approaches usually maintain that individual emotion words plot affective experience within a continuous, gradient space with fuzzy boundaries (a *circumplex*), reflecting various measures of the core dimensions (Barrett, 1998; Barrett & Russell, 1999; Feldman, 1995a, 1995b; Plutchik & Conte, 1997; Posner, Russell, & Peterson, 2005; Russell, 1979, 1980; Russell & Barrett, 1999). Barrett and Russell's work on the dimensional aspects of affect led to the development of *psychological constructivist* approaches to emotion, the most prominent intellectual competitor to basic/discrete emotion theories today.

Though psychological construction can be approached in different ways (Barrett, 2013), the most important (by far) emerges from the work of Barrett and colleagues, whose evolving model has been called *conceptual act theory* (Barrett, 2006b; Barrett, Wilson-Mendenhall, & Barsalou, 2015; Lindquist & Barrett, 2008), the *theory of constructed emotion* (Barrett, 2017a, 2017b), and, most recently, the *constructed mind approach* (Barrett & Lida, 2024). While it is impossible to do justice to the enormous amount of literature this research program has generated, its current outlook basically argues that the human mind is a constantly simulating entity that uses predictive computational principles to construct emotional meaning from the sensory signals it receives from the body and environment (Barrett & Lida, 2024; see also Lindquist, 2013; Russell, 2009; and the citations in this paragraph). For our purposes, the key point is that what folk psychology calls "emotion" has no inherent biological meaning in this model; discrete "emotions" as typically understood do not actually exist in nature, and thus are in no way universal, but rather reflect a *"population of events* whose physical features will be *highly* variable, and whose functional features will be variable" (Barrett & Lida, 2024, p. 365; see Barrett, 2006a, 2012, 2022; Lindquist et al., 2013).

Building on the skepticism of earlier scholars (J. M. Carroll & Russell, 1996; Fridlund, 1994; Russell, 1994; Russell & Fehr, 1987), constructivists take particular aim at BET's claims that facial expressions of emotion are universally produced and recognized; they argue that these conclusions are based on a faulty methodology that does not reflect the actual conditions in which emotions are expressed. In contrast, their experiments and research point to positive evidence that context and language labels vitally facilitate the perception of emotion, that different cultures perceive emotions differently, that the same emotional expression can signal a multiplicity of emotions, and that the so-called basic emotions do not actually generate predicted facial expressions in a reliable way (Aviezer, Hassin, Ryan, et al., 2008; Aviezer et al., 2008; Barrett, Mesquita, & Gendron, 2011; Barrett et al., 2019; Brooks et al., 2017; Crivelli et al., 2016; Durán & Fernández-Dols, 2021; Durán, Reisenzein, & Fernández-Dols, 2017; Fang et al., 2022; Gendron, 2017; Gendron et al., 2014; Gendron, Crivelli, & Barrett, 2018; Hess & Hareli, 2019; Israelashvili, Hassin, & Aviezer, 2019; Jack et al., 2012; Lee & Anderson, 2016; Lindquist et al., 2006; Nelson & Russell, 2013). Constructivists similarly argue that empirical findings do not support the claim that discrete emotions have a specific physiological signature, given the robust evidence that different instances of the supposedly same emotion can trigger different types of bodily responses (Barrett, Ochsner, & Gross, 2007; Chentsova-Dutton et al., 2020; Hoemann et al., 2020; Lang, 2014; Mauss & Robinson, 2009; Mendes, 2016; Mendes & Park, 2014; Siegel et al., 2018; Tsai et al., 2002).

Beyond psychological constructivism, other psychologists similarly resist a thoroughly universalist approach to emotion. Some, for instance, point to the fact that mainstream psychology draws many of its conclusions – including its universalist conclusions – by research emerging from a WEIRD (white, educated, industrial, rich, and democratic) context, a demographic that hardly represents the world's population (Arnett, 2008; Henrich, Heine, & Norenzayan, 2010). While the field of *cross-cultural* psychology, we saw in the last section, is (in part) alert to similarities in different social populations – including how universal principles may lay behind apparent cultural variation – the field of *cultural* psychology, writes one of its founders, emphasizes "psychological diversity, rather than psychological uniformity" (Shweder, 2007, p. 827): It is "the study of the way cultural traditions and social practices regulate, express, transform, and permute the human psyche, resulting less in psychic unity for humankind than in ethnic divergences in mind, self, and emotion" (Shweder, 1990, p. 1). Different cultures, it is argued, have different kinds of psychologies (Markus & Kitayama, 1991), and this has obvious implications for emotions, which emerge not as universal phenomenon but as contingent cultural constructions (Boiger et al., 2018; De Leersnyder, Mesquita, & Boiger, 2021; Mesquita, Boiger, & De Leersnyder, 2016, 2017). It has been said that *emotion* (as it is usually understood) may not even be a useful theoretical construct to consider mental states across human populations generally (Shweder, 2004).

Cultural psychologists thus argue that "emotions ... are neither natural nor universal" (Mesquita, 2022), and their research explicitly considers that the meaning of certain emotions (like *shame* or *humiliated fury*) are not culturally universal (Kirchner et al., 2018; Kollareth, Fernández-Dols, & Russell, 2018).

Work on emotion in cultural psychology thus often falls under the broad umbrella of social constructivist approaches, as in Mesquita and Boiger's *sociodynamic model* – which, seeing them as "largely functional to the sociocultural environment in which they occur," argues that emotions are "dynamic systems that emerge from the interactions and relationships in which they take place" (Mesquita & Boiger, 2014, p. 298; see Boiger & Mesquita, 2012a, 2012b, 2015). In its emphasis on population variance, cultural psychology also shares terrain with the more specific subfield of indigenous psychologies (Ciofalo, 2019; Kim, Yang, & Hwang, 2006; Paredes-Canilao et al., 2015). Tending to indigenous perspectives entails a "movement from investigation of psychological universals to study of culture as a psychological system [with] a bottom-up approach that builds theoretical views based on local phenomena" (Keith, 2019, p. 10); this rejection of universalism is seen in work on emotion, as in studies of how affect is particularly understood in the indigenous thought systems of West Sumatra (Heider, 2011), China (Sundararajan, 2015), India (Bilimoria & Wenta, 2015), and Tanzania (Hoemann, 2024). Finally, we saw in the last section how evolutionary psychology has been used to underpin universalist approaches, but there have recently emerged more explicitly constructivist approaches to the evolution of emotion (Bliss-Moreau, Williams, & Karaskiewicz, 2021; Lindquist et al., 2022); these models, which reflect the fact that evolutionary thinking has always been a component of psychological construction, view discrete emotion categories as concepts that have emerged from a process of cultural evolution (see Mesoudi, 2016).

Constructivist theorists may acknowledge limited universality in certain particular aspects of emotion – that is, the basic psychological "ingredients" that give rise to emotion may be a typical part of human mental architecture, and there may be a general regularity in how people categorize the co-occurring response patterns of certain emotion episodes – but the more salient point is that they see the experience of emotion as "primarily a subjective interpretation constructed within the mind[,] rather than reflecting the objectively measurable effects of a dedicated neural program's activation" (Shiota, Camras, & Adolphs, 2023, p. 431). As such, their position is usually thought of as an anti-universalist approach to emotion that stands in contrast to the universalism of basic and discrete theories of emotion.

## Neuroscience

Though much work in affective neuroscience, we saw in the last section, is premised on emotional universalism, this is not absolute, as constructivist approaches to the brain have also generated important research. An early example of constructivist neuroscience is the work of Brothers (1997), who emphasized the social embeddedness of human brains; taking issue with the outlook of LeDoux and Damasio, she argued that the "failures" of neuroscientists to "find emotion in hardware of the brain . . . prove[s] that the isolated-mind concept of emotion must be discarded" (p. 111). In the twenty-first century, however, opposition to the universalist perspective of affective neuroscience has come primarily from proponents of the constructivist theory of emotion championed by Barrett; this outlook challenges the conclusions that neural "signatures" can be discovered for discrete emotions, arguing instead that "emotion categories are unlikely to have distinct and innate physical correlates within the brain that are replicable across different contexts" (Clark-Polner et al., 2016, p. 153).

Early in the development of psychological constructivist theory, Barrett et al. (2007) argued that there is a "tremendous amount of evidence that is inconsistent" with the idea that certain discrete emotions are "biologically basic and derive from architecturally and chemically distinct circuits that are hard coded into the human brain at birth" (p. 297); in their view, "the evolutionary legacy to the newborn is not a set of modular emotion circuits that are hardwired into the subcortical features of the mammalian brain but may be, instead, a set of mechanisms that compute core affect and allow affective learning, as well as those that allow conceptual learning and categorization" (p. 305). For such scholars, neuroimaging evidence suggests that "many of the brain regions consistently activated during emotional experiences and perceptions show consistent activation in meta-analyses of other mental phenomena," meaning that "brain regions are implementing basic psychological operations that are not specific to any emotion per se, or even to the category 'emotion'" (Lindquist & Barrett, 2012, p. 535). In 2012, a much-cited meta-analysis from the same research team "failed to locate a specific brain basis for discrete emotion categories," finding instead that "common brain activations exist across emotion categories" and "the bulk of the empirical evidence is more consistent with the hypothesis that emotions emerge from the interplay of more basic psychological operations" (Lindquist et al., 2012, pp. 141, 142; see also Wilson-Mendenhall, Barrett, & Barsalou, 2013). Others agreed that there is "strong evidence against the existence of super-specialized macro-anatomical structures for representations of single emotion categories (e.g. amygdala for fear)" (Guillory & Bujarski, 2014, p. 1887) and that "emotion categories are not contained within any one region or system, but are represented as configurations across multiple brain networks" (Wager et al., 2015, p. 1); a growing number of studies from the Barrett research team and others generally reflect that neural activity for emotion is distributed across the whole brain and overlaps with other cognitive processes (Huang et al., 2018; Raz et al., 2016; Touroutoglou et al., 2015; Zhou, 2021).

Other research supporting a constructivist view suggests the importance of contextual classification and categorization at the neural level (Brooks et al., 2017; Brooks et al., 2019) and that using the predetermined "labels" of folk emotion already distorts our interpretation of neural evidence (Azari et al., 2020). Most recently, discrete emotion theories have been challenged by pointing to the process of neural degeneracy, the fact that "instances of an emotion (e.g. fear) are created by multiple spatiotemporal patterns in varying populations of neurons" (Barrett, 2017b, p. 3); the fact that "multiple functional neural network patterns can result in instances of the same emotion category" is said to confound the notion that discrete emotions have particular neural signatures (Doyle et al., 2022, p. 996).

Though constructivists acknowledge that studies in nonhuman animals have found dedicated neural circuits that control behaviors such as escaping, freezing, and fighting, they suggest that "there are a number of arguments for why a neural circuit for a behavior cannot be considered a neural circuit for an emotion *per se*" – for example, that an animal might variously flee, freeze, or fighting during an ostensible "fear" state seems to complicate the notion that a single neural mechanism controls what we understand as the emotion of fear (Touroutoglou et al., 2015, p. 1257). They also object to how discrete emotion theorists interpret the findings of techniques like multivoxel pattern analysis, arguing that such research still indicates that "when it comes to the observed pattern for any single emotion category, variation is the norm"; that the physical correlates of emotion are "highly variable within an emotion category from instance to instance" is taken to mean that there is no neural signature of discrete emotion, as many universalist theorists have historically predicted (Barrett & Satpute, 2019, p. 12; see Clark-Polner, Johnson, & Barrett, 2017).

## Sociology

In the previous section, we saw how sociologists of emotion can have great sympathy for the universalist outlook – but this does not mean, in turn, that the positivist approach is self-evidently dominant in the field. Longo (2020), in fact, argues that it is best practice for sociologists to explicitly deemphasize any presumed innate universality of emotion, and others seem to agree. "In sociology," it was said not too long ago, "we have been reluctant to overcome our historic tendency to associate all biology with reductionism" (Franks, 2010, p. 2) – and even more recently, "the idea that emotions are primarily biological phenomena" has been called an "obstacle to the sociological study of emotions" (Harris, 2015, p. 3) – so it makes sense that the positivist emphasis on the physiological foundations of emotion has not fully taken hold. Turner and Stets (2005) even suggest that the sociology of emotion has been conventionally framed in constructivist terms: "for most sociologists, emotions are socially constructed in the sense that what people feel is conditioned by socialization into culture and by participation in social structures" (p. 2). Indeed, as Lively (2024) has recently put it, "the bulk of sociological scholarship on emotion," irrespective of specific focus, tends to ask questions like "how do historically and culturally specific norms influence the experience and expression of emotion ... and what role do emotions play in reifying and disrupting cultural and social constraints" – inquiries obviously premised on the fact that certain vital aspects of emotion are shaped by culturally and historically contingent social forces (p. 289). There is thus a rich tradition of constructivism in sociology, which runs in parallel to the positivist scholarship reviewed in Section 1.

The constructivist position fundamentally suggests that "human emotionality is shaped by the ensemble of social relationships that bind human beings to one another" (Denzin, 1990, p. 90). Emotions are "aspects of a specific culture and social context which determine when, and in which social circumstances, they may be properly manifested and how they should be managed"; they are seen as "socially defined in the sense that it is the social that sets their meaning and normative standards that regulate their expression and management, [while] the biological component is reduced to the organic mechanism which trigger emotions" (Longo, 2020, pp. 4, 43). This outlook is seen primarily in what Bericat (2016) describes as *cultural theories*, which "see emotion not as mere biological responses but as *social feelings*" (p. 499). With this approach, constructivist sociologists emphasize processes such as emotional labeling and strategies of emotional management – that is, ways in which the expression and experience of emotion are shaped by contextual forces.

The constructivist tradition of modern emotion sociology is most usually said to inaugurate with Hochschild (1979), whose work on emotion management came to emphasize "*secondary acts* performed upon the ongoing nonreflective stream of primary experience" – that is, "how social factors affect what people think and do about what they feel (i.e. acts of assessment and management)" (p. 552; see also Hochschild, 1983b). At the same time, Shott (1979) began to focus on both "the socialization of emotion, which generates variability in affective experience across cultures [and] the construction of emotions by the actor, a process greatly influenced by situational definitions and social norms" (p. 1318). A few years later, Thoits (1985) argued that "only through language do we know *what* we feel, and implicitly, why" – that is, when "a cultural label is placed on a conjunction of situational cues physiological sensations, and bodily gestures" (pp. 232–233) – and she later affirmed that "along with most sociologists, I assume that emotions are not simply innate, biophysiological phenomena," because "considerable variability exists historically and cross-culturally in the situational causes, experience, meaning, display, and regulation of emotions, including basic ones" (1989, p. 319). Perhaps most stridently, Gordon's work on emotional labeling (1990) maintains that "emotion should be viewed as an 'open system' in which the entire combination of elements is socially constructed, rather than a closed system in which society merely activates or stimulates the fixed connections" (p. 153; see Gordon, 1981).

And there is, of course, plenty of more recent scholarship that takes an anti-universalist approach. Longo (2020), for example, acknowledges that "approaches which consider emotions as universal, transcultural and homogeneous, based as they are on some essentialist conception of human action, are endowed with a cogent persuasiveness" – but he begins his study of emotions, society, and the self by arguing that "the very possibility of a sociology of emotions lies not in homologies but in differences," in the sense that "if emotions were experienced and managed in the same way across historical times, cultures and the different strata of the same society, any attempt at a sociology of emotions would be frustrating" (p. 1).

## Anthropology

Constructivism, we have already seen, has played a vital role in how anthropologists have historically theorized emotion. Constructivist accounts have emphasized several categories of evidence: the "celebrated counter examples" (Beatty, 2014, p. 546) of cultures that seemingly don't experience certain basic emotion profiles, such as sadness for Tahitians (Levy, 1973) or anger for the Utku Iniut (Briggs, 1970); cultures that experience emotions that are seemingly foreign and untranslatable to the Western tradition, such as the Ilongot *liget* (M. Z. Rosaldo, 1980), the Balinese *lek* (Geertz, 1973), or the Japanese *amae* (Lebra, 1976); or cultures that seem to understand the fundamental evaluative framework of emotion to reside beyond the Western sense of interiority, such as the Ifaluk, who see it in terms of situational events (Lutz, 1982), or Samoans, who see it in terms of social goodness (Gerber, 1975).

As noted in the previous section, the Boasian emphasis on the psychic unity of humankind did not lead early twentieth-century anthropologists to seek patterns of cultural uniformity; instead, its rejection of cultural evolution models (and the hierarchization of cultures that they underpinned) resulted in a relativistic interest in the particularities of culture and personality, as evidenced in the work of Mead, Benedict, and Bateson (Bateson & Mead, 1942; Benedict, 1935; Mead, 1928, 1930, 1935; see Beatty, 2019; Stodulka, 2017). The anti-universalist bent is suggested by Mead's study of "three primitive societies," which led her "to conclude that human nature is almost unbelievably malleable, responding accurately and contrastingly to contrasting cultural conditions" (1935, p. 280). Other early scholarship, such as that of Labarre (1947) and Birdwhistell (1970), challenged the notion that nonverbal emotion cues like gestures and facial expressions were actually as universal as the Darwinian camp claimed. In the middle of the century, relativistic anthropology was further invigorated by the research of C. Geertz, with vast implications for the understanding of emotion; across a variety of studies, he argued that "not only ideas, but emotions too are cultural artifacts in man" (1962, p. 735), that "the passions are as cultural as [social institutions]" (1980, p. 124), and that "our ideas, our values, our acts, even our emotions, are, like our nervous system itself, cultural products" (1966, p. 114). Given his emphasis on emotion as a cultural concept, the attack on universality was explicit: to attribute meaning to "universal properties of the human mind," he argued, "is to pretend a science that does not exist and imagine a reality that cannot be found" (1973, p. 20).

The work of C. Geertz paved the way for the heyday of constructivist anthropological accounts in the 1970s, 1980s, and 1990s, most notably advanced by Lutz (1982, 1986, 1988; Abu-Lughod & Lutz, 1990; Lutz & White, 1986). This work, she reflected some decades later, "relativized, historicized, and contextualized both the emotions or emotionality and the Euro-American psychological science that asserted itself as at the helm of understanding emotion" (Lutz, 2017, p. 182). As this suggests, the approach is particularly premised on the correction of an alleged Eurocentric essentialism in previous anthropology, which sought emotions "in the supposedly more permanent structures of human existence – in spleens, souls, genes, human nature, and individual psychology, rather than in history, culture, ideology, and temporary human purposes"; accordingly, to look critically "at the Euroamerican construction of emotion is to unmask the ways in which that schema unconsciously serves as a normative device for judging the mental health of culturally different peoples" (Lutz, 1986, pp. 287, 288). Similarly, it was noted in the last section that some anthropologists appealed to the presumed universality of empathy in their work on emotion, but constructivist accounts of this period often explicitly denounced this practice; Lynch (1990), for example, advises that we must "reject empathy as a naive and ethnocentric practice, a form of Western imperialism over the emotions of the Other" (p. 17; see also C. Geertz, 1975).

In "going beyond [a] psychobiological framework to include concerns with emotion's social relational, communicative, and cultural aspects" (Lutz & White, 1986, p. 405), this research particularly emphasizes the role of language in the construction of emotion; many of these studies "approach emotion through language and understand language as inescapably and fundamentally social," meaning that "emotion can be said to be *created in*, rather than shaped by, speech in the sense that it is postulated as an entity in language where its meaning to social actors is also elaborated" (Abu-Lughod, & Lutz, pp. 10, 12). More specifically, Lutz's study of the Ifaluk people "treat[s] emotion as an ideological practice rather than as a thing to discovered or an essence to be distilled," in order to "demonstrate how emotional meaning is fundamentally structured by particular cultural systems and particular social and material environments" (1988, pp. 4, 5). Similar research includes that of Abu-Lughod (1986), which emphasizes "the cultural construction of the sentiments" (p. 206); Grima (1992), which argues most fundamentally that "emotion is culturally constructed rather than universal" (p. 6); and especially M. Rosaldo, which resists the anthropological tendency "to view affective life more as a 'sign' that points to social rule than as itself a sphere of meaning that [is] public and socially significant"(1980, p. 35), and affirms that "affects, whatever their similarities, are no more similar than the societies in which we live" (1984, p. 145).

Although emotion is somewhat less of an anthropological focus in the twenty-first century, many scholars today still adopt a fundamentally constructivist outlook. Illouz and Wilf (2009), for example, in their more recent study of love, affirm that "the anthropology of emotion has successfully refuted [the] view – hitherto dominant – that emotions are physiological responses to situations, which in turn make them universal invariants of human action"; they thus align themselves with the long research tradition (following C. Geertz) that has "showed repeatedly that emotions are shaped, through and through, by cultural meanings, and in particular by cultural conceptions of the person" (p. 124).

## Philosophy

As stated in Section 1, many contemporary philosophers employ notions of affect programs or biologically "basic" emotions in their analysis. This does not mean, however, that there are no dissenters. Harré (1986), in a collection devoted to the social construction of emotion, argued that "the overwhelming evidence of cultural diversity and cognitive differentiation in the emotions of mankind has become so obvious that a new consensus is developing around the idea of social construction" – a consensus that upturns the "universalistic implications" of earlier research (p. 3; see also Harrré, 2000). In the same volume, Armon-Jones (1986b) explicitly lays out "the thesis of construction-ism": "emotions are characterized by attitudes such as beliefs, judgements and desires, the contents of which are not natural, but are determined by the systems of cultural belief, value, and moral value of particular communities" (p. 33; see also Armon-Jones, 1986a). Finally, at one point in his career, Solomon (1984) explicitly opposed the understanding that emotions "can be presumed a priori (and falsely) to be more or less the same in all human beings": he rejects the "familiar but fallacious" view that "emotions can therefore be taken to be more or less universal human phenomena," leading him to the thesis that "emotions are to be construed as cultural acquisitions, determined by the circumstances and concepts of a particular culture as well as, or rather much more than, by the functions of biology and, more specifically, neurology" (pp. 239–240). Solomon seems to have adopted a more hybrid position later in his career, but continued to maintain that philosophers must not a priori assume emotional universality (see Solomon, 1995).

While emotional constructivism per se seems less popular with twenty-first-century philosophers, contemporary thinkers do usually grant that social and cultural context is an important part of emotional experience. Finally, it must again be noted that many philosophers argue that neither the folk category *emotion* nor specific emotion categories (i.e. *anger*) have natural boundaries – but this does not mean, as we saw in Section 1, that they reject the possibility that certain emotional responses (i.e. *affect program fear*) are biologically natural and thus universal.

## History

In the last forty years, the history of emotion has emerged as a vibrant research cluster (for overviews see; Barclay, 2020, 2021b; Boddice, 2018, 2020b, 2024; Knatz, 2023; Matt & Stearns, 2013; Plamper, 2015; Rosenwein & Cristiani, 2017; Schnell, 2021). "Historians of emotion," it has been recently said, "can, with confidence, settle debates about universalism" (Boddice, 2019, p. 1994), and the boldness of this statement reflects the fact that historians are essentially unified in their outlook on the question of emotional universality.

The "key premise of the history of emotions is that emotion varies across time and place and so has a history that can be explored by scholars" – so unsurprisingly, this naturally positions virtually all historians to take an anti-universalist stance in their research (Barclay, 2021b, p. 457). Historians occasionally suggest that their work is premised on an essentially shared understanding of emotion – Eustace (2008), for example, writes that "we are able to analyze eighteenth-century emotion today only because of a shared physiology of feeling that stretches over the centuries" (p. 12) – but this is generally not the focus of historical research (nor is it the focus of Eustace). Three decades ago, Danziger (1990) noted that many historians of the day had "overlook[ed] the possibility that the very objects of psychological discourse, and not just opinions about them, have changed radically in the course of history" (p. 336); as the contemporary field of emotion history began to develop in the intervening years, scholars took this caution to heart. "To put it simply," Dodman (2021) has recently argued, "unchanging, basic emotions hard-wired by evolutionary processes go against the very idea of a *history* of emotions" (p. 17). It is thus with good reason, he continues, that "most historians stick to tried and tested social constructivist positions"; though many "historians of emotion have been very conscious of work in psychology, biology and neuroscience," the emphasis is almost entirely on the scientific work that "provides models for imagining the body as plastic and historical, as much as universal" (Barclay, 2021a, p. 114). Historians of emotion thus overwhelmingly agree with Rosenwein (2001) that "emotions themselves are extremely plastic" and that "it is very hard to maintain, except at an abstract level, that emotions are everywhere the same" (p. 231). "In this field," Knatz (2023) thus observes, "past emotions ... are thought of as *qualitatively* different, ontologically divergent over time" – and there is little room for notions of universality (p. 275). Accordingly, in history of emotion work, constructivist models of emotions are routinely held up for praise (Boddice, 2020a, 2020b; Bound Alberti, 2018; Eustace et al., 2012; Reddy, 2020; Rosenwein, 2021; Tepora, 2020), while the basic and discrete models of "Neo-Darwinists, hard-line geneticists, behaviourists [and] biological determinists" are subjected to fierce critique (Boddice, 2018, p. 46).

"Recent theoreticians of the history of emotion," Tepora (2020) notes, have "vigorously defended the malleability of emotions over time and across cultures by rejecting the universalism of basic emotions," and a sampling of statements from contemporary scholars confirms this assessment (p. 98). Rosenwein, for example, elsewhere notes that "universalist and presentist views of the emotions [are] problematic enough" that emotion history is a necessary field (2010, p. 10), and it is "very unlikely that emotions are invariable" (2016, p. 2). Plamper (2015) states that "what is universal [in emotion] amounts to a molehill when compared to the mountain of data on cultural difference" – and besides, "the universal is often uninteresting" (p. 33). Warning against "the temptation toward the universality of emotional phenomena," Boddice (2017) suggests that "to say that emotions change over time is incompatible with claims that there is something fundamentally transcendent or basic about (some) emotions"; accordingly, he affirms that "the history of emotions implicitly challenges basic-emotions models [and] should explicitly do so" (pp. 11, 12).

Bound Alberti (2018) writes that "Ekman's reductionist biological model has been criticized by more nuanced theorists who demonstrate that rather than being universal, emotions are developed within complex power relations, and through the lenses of disciplinary classifications that are themselves historically specific" (p. 243). Reddy (2020) believes that the "weaknesses" of BET are "in fact so obvious that one must ask why this theory has had such a long life" (p. 168). And Dixon (2020) denounces the "essentialism, ethnocentrism and anachronism" that arises when one considers "unchanging, universal emotion-[s]" (pp. 11, 3). Indeed, it has recently been said that the entire field of emotion history "sees itself as a reaction to universalistic and biological conceptions of emotions" (Schnell, 2021, p. 25).

## Linguistics

In the previous section, we saw how a universalist approach to language dominated the field of linguistics in the second half of the twentieth century – but this was not always the case. In 1969, it was actually said that "the prevailing doctrine of American linguistics and anthropologists has, in this century, been that of extreme linguistic relativity," meaning that "each language is semantic-ally arbitrary relative to every other language" – according to this outlook, "the search for semantic universals is fruitless in principle" (Berlin & Kay, 1969, pp. 1–2). And there has been a more recent general challenge to universalism, with at least some researchers claiming that "the idea of a single underlying linguistic system different only in surface realization seems increasingly unlikely" (Majid, 2012, p. 432). Evans and Levinson (2009), for example, argued that "languages differ so fundamentally from one another at every level of description (sound, grammar, lexicon, meaning) that it is very hard to find any single structural property they share"; accordingly, there are "vanish-ingly few universals of language," and linguistic universality is just a myth that has endured despite "a massive accumulation of counter evidence" (pp. 429, 430).

Most famously developed by Sapir (1921) and Whorf (1956), theories of linguistic relativity maintain that the properties of language shape human thought, to some degree or another. Extreme versions of the so-called Sapir-Whorf hypothesis seem unlikely – people are self-evidently able to conceptualize and understand concepts that are not linguistically present in their native language – but more flexible notions of linguistic relativity, which still reflect "just how profoundly the variation in languages can influence forms of cognition" (Downey & Gillett, 2023, p. 694), give rise to the notion of *emotional linguistic relativity*, the possibility that "the way we feel may depend, at least in part, upon the language[s] we speak" (Ponsonnet, 2022, p. 1033). Consistent with psychological constructivist theories, such a perspective argues that "the way we [linguistically] conceptualize emotions is likely to influence the way we experience them" (p. 1054). This outlook is shared by many linguistic anthropologists, who embrace cultural particularism and believe that the language of emotion is "inseparable from culture, and as likely to shape as be shaped by mind" (Wilce, 2014, p. 79; see also Besnier, 1990). Bamberg (1997a), for example, began by "view[ing] emotions from the starting point of language" – that is, "how language forms *reflect* or *construct* what is commonly taken as an emotion" (p. 209) – to develop a "linguistic-constructionist" approach that inverts the "traditional, realist picture of the relationship between emotions, cognitions and language" (1997b, pp. 310, 335).

Critiques of linguistic emotional universality also take other forms. The very field of historical linguistics, for example, reflects the fact that "people's words for emotions have been and will be alive throughout their histories, reflecting changing ideas of what emotions are, how they relate to each other, how they relate to other concepts, and how they affect us" (Tissari, 2017, p. 93). In terms of metaphor, we have seen how conceptual metaphor theory posits the ubiquity of certain primary emotional metaphors based on universal physiology; however, evidence suggests that different languages (such as English and Hebrew) vary in the way and extent to which somatic metaphors are employed (Kidron & Kuzar, 2002). Even seemingly stable metaphors are not always cross-culturally consistent; for example, a recent study of Mlabri (a language of Thailand and Laos) shows emotional mappings of DOWN as desirable and UP as undesirable, confounding the "commonly reported HAPPY IS UP metaphor [that] is said to link to universal bodily correlates of emotion" (Wnuk & Ito, 2021, p. 195). These metaphors are "grounded in the bodily experience of positive low-arousal states," suggesting that in their metaphoric usage "cultures draw on the available sensorimotor correlates of emotion in distinct ways." And it has been argued that the cognitive linguist positing of primary metaphors based on fundamental experience and physiology is an "ahistorical method [that] obscures the possible role of cultural traditions as a source of emotion concepts" (Geeraerts, 2006, p. 227). Beyond differences in metaphor, the social construction of emotion language may be particularly indicated by multilingual speakers, in the sense that "in any pair of languages, specific emotion concepts may overlap completely, partially, or not at all"; those adept in multiple languages thus report tension and difficulty in negotiating certain emotion concepts across languages, leading to the hypothesis that "bilinguals' concepts may, in some cases, be distinct from those of monolingual speakers" (Pavlenko, 2008, pp. 152, 147; see also Pavlenko, 2005, 2006). Above all, many skeptical linguists argue that emotion theorists often "seem unaware of absolutising their own language (with its built-in culture and concepts), i.e. of making universal claims on the basis of language-specific categories" (Dewaele, 2010, p. 18).

Finally, psychologists in the constructivist tradition have also conducted complementary research on language – unsurprisingly, given that language seems to be "especially important to the acquisition and use of [the] conceptual knowledge" that underpins the theory of constructed emotion (Doyle & Lindquist, 2018, p. 62). Gendron, Lindquist, Barsalou, and Barrett (2012) argue that "emotion words provide an important (although often unrecognized) context in emotion perception" (p. 321). Doyle and Lindquist (2018) find that "emotion words support the acquisition of new conceptual knowledge that then biase[s] subsequent perceptual memory for emotional facial actions" (p. 72). Satpute and Lindquist (2021) found that neural processes associated with language are also involved with emotion, leading to their constructivist conclusion that "language shapes emotional experience" (p. 216). And most recently, Ogren and Sandhofer's (2022) study of emotion labeling in children suggested "language may in fact be important for emotion understanding and therefore that linguistic differences across cultures may lead to differences in emotion perception cross-culturally" (p. 175).

## Literary and Cultural Studies

As noted in the previous section, modern scholars have largely overturned the long-held interpretive belief in the existence of literary universals. "In many areas of literary studies today," Gallese and Wojciehowski (2018) note, "and for the past several decades, the idea of universals has been heavily challenged . . . [t]here are persistent and ongoing concerns that any claims to universality will be ensconced as social or cultural norms that delegitimize or stigmatize persons or groups whose experiences do not conform to those norms" (n.p.). We may consider the case of Shakespeare, who has long been considered the quintessential example of a universal poet. In recent years, researchers have demonstrated that the apparent global appeal of Shakespeare owes no small part to the coercive dynamics of imperialism, as the playwright was purposefully utilized in the British colonial education system to Anglicize native inhabitants of colonized lands. Shakespeare's reputation as "universal" thus reflects how a conscious political program disingenuously enshrined a white, male, European viewpoint as culturally normative (to the determent of native perspectives), leading many literary scholars today to see Shakespeare's supposed universality as little more than a racist myth historically deployed as "an instrument of colonial hegemony" (Weissbourd, 2023, p. 207).

In general, universality has extremely low currency in modern literary studies, so scholars devote little explicit time advancing a nonuniversalist theory of emotion: a constructivist position is rather assumed. A typical account can be found in Scott (2019), who introduces his analysis of emotion in postcolonial literature by affirming that "I am not suggesting, of course, that emotion can be easily universalized . . . quite the opposite: I view emotion not as the product of some ahistorical psychic essence, but as a 'felt response' to specific social, political, and economic forces" (p. 27). The "of course" indicates the extent to which a universalist perspective on emotion would be unusual in contemporary research on literature; typical sympathies are much more apt to align with Gross's (2010) sense that "emotional encounters that we might attribute to our biologically ground intuitions must always be considered in a larger political context where the status of social institutions are at stake" (pp. 47–48). There, is, however, a small amount of work that directly argues against the universality of emotion; in their treatment of neuroscience and literature, for example, both Armstrong (2020) and Comer and Taggart (2021) ground their understanding of emotion in the work of Barrett and generally adopt a constructivist perspective.

Because of its poststructuralist genealogy, cultural theory is heavily suspicious of biological determinism and universalizing tendencies. Ahmed (2004), arguably the most prominent and influential cultural theorist of affect, explicitly announces "a critique of the assumption that emotions are innate or biological (p. 17). Leys (2017, 2021) forcefully criticizes affect theorists for their regular use of universalizing scientists like Ekman – but, as noted in the previous section, even affect theorists who use such science for philosophical speculation would probably not consider themselves emotional universalists in the same way that a psychologist or neuroscientist might.

## 3 Hybrid Models and Compromise Positions: Pathways for the Future

As the previous two sections have demonstrated, virtually every major scholarly discipline that concerns itself with emotion has been divided on the question of whether human emotionality should be understood, in one way or another, as meaningfully "universal." Yet, a decade ago, Wetherell (2012) noted that the "packaging of affect through the debate between 'basic emotions' and 'social construction'" has been a major "wrong-turn" in emotion research (p. 17) – in the sense that it has underpinned the "increasingly sterile division of labour between the biological and the cultural" (p. 19) – and there is indeed now a feeling among many researchers that it is vital to find some sort of compromise position. This section describes some of the ways that scholars have attempted to do so, with models that account for the apparently inescapable fact that there are aspects of both regularity and variance in human emotion.

## Assessing the Debate

Before proceeding, however, it is important to reflect briefly on the central contention between universalists and anti-universalists, now that both sides of the debate have been presented. One consistent barrier to research, it must be said, is that partisans of each position will too often display a reluctance to engage the other with a general good faith, leading to a polarized entrenchment where distorted claims about theoretical opponents are tossed back and forth, while important unfavorable evidence is conveniently ignored. Boddice (2024), for example, has recently written that "the methods of the universalists have been found wanting on numberless occasions," yet "the universalist school has not substantially engaged with any of this, but rather carried on regardless" (p. xi). While this is certainly true in particular cases, I believe it is somewhat misleading as a general statement, and (more importantly) an identical charge can be levied at anti-universalists: many constructivists refuse to engage with the ongoing developments of their theoretical adversaries, choosing instead to overwhelmingly focus on how the supposed refutation of a single research program (that of Ekman) on a single aspect of emotion (expression recognition) is enough to unequivocally and absolutely discredit all theories of basic or discrete emotion, despite the amassed evidence for patterns of regularity and consistency in different emotion domains across cultures. Indeed, many constructivists devote their time to attacking what Shiota (2024) calls the "cartoon" version of BET, an oversimplified and essentially invented model of discrete emotion that is not actually maintained by any current researchers in the field (p. 313).

In this sense, basic and discrete emotion theories in 2024 have evolved to be significantly more complex and nuanced than the more rigid, traditional classic BET of the late twentieth century – that is, the BET that is most often held up for critique. Constructivist theorists, we have seen, have particularly attacked BET by homing on flaws in early emotional recognition studies – but, as Keltner, Sauter, et al. (2019) more recently note, the "field has moved beyond relying exclusively on forced choice labeling of expressions, and progress is being made in understanding how social perceivers infer intentions, motives, action tendencies, and relational properties of signaler and perceiver in brief expressions of emotion" (p. 135). To this end, Keltner and Cordaro (2017) ground their research in basic emotion theory, but argue that there is evidence for discrete multimodal expression patterns in far more emotions than the "Big 6" of traditional BET; Cordaro et al. (2018), for example, identified "cross-cultural *core patterns* of expressive behavior [for] 22 emotions [and] a gradient of universality for the 22 emotions" (p. 75; see also Cordaro et al., 2020; Cowen & Keltner, 2020). In terms of the brain, Celeghin, Diano, Bagnis, Viola, and Tamietto (2017) argue that "evidence in favor of the neurobiological underpinnings of basic emotions outweighs dismissive approaches," when we realize that a theory of discrete emotions doesn't strictly demand (as is sometimes claimed) a traditional one-to-one localization between anatomical structures and emotion signatures: "moving the focus of neuroscientific research from individual brain regions to networks, and from the simplistic region based one-to-one localizations to more sophisticated network-based one-to-many relationships between neural structure and function seems to prefigure a more modern and neurobiologically plausible approach to the study of basic emotions," and will indeed prove that BET is "still tenable and heuristically seminal" (pp. 1, 8; see also Scarantino, 2012c). A number of researchers seem to agree, emphasizing that basic emotions demonstrate a "discreteness ... best understood as widespread, system-level patterned activity, rather than selective regional or systemic engagement during specific emotions" – that is, "neurophysiological data support the view of multiple discrete emotion systems that are organized in a distributed fashion across the brain, with no clear one-to-one mapping between emotions and brain regions" (Nummenmaa & Saarimäki, 2019, pp. 7, 3; see also Saarimäki et al., 2018).

Thus, basic and discrete emotion theory is still a thriving and viable research program, which has not (despite what is sometimes said) been overturned by the rise of modern constructivist theories. Scarantino (2014, 2018; see also Scarantino & Griffiths, 2011), for example, has worked on a "*new* BET" that reflects constructionist critiques (2015, p. 334). He argues that "basic emotions are evolved programs that coordinate more basic ingredients such as facial muscle responses, autonomic blood flow, subjective experiences, respiratory and vocal change, motor patterns, thoughts, memories, images"; what "unites the ingredients of a basic emotion together is an evolved and specialized basic emotion program," which "was selected to coordinate organismic resources to deal successfully with fundamental life tasks such as avoiding dangers, removing obstacles, coping losses" (p. 335). In the new BET, "what is universal when it comes to basic emotions are first and foremost the evolved programs that run them" – but variability in *manifestation* of basic emotion is to be expected, because these programs need to be context-dependent and flexible to address natural variation in the fundamental life tasks they are designed to address

(p. 336). Accordingly, the theory crucially posits that there will be a variety of *functional variants* in basic emotion manifestation, that is, different ways that the ingredients of emotion will specifically present while still "preserving the task-oriented nature of the response" (p. 340). Reflecting this flexibility, basic emotions in this model thus become "*input-output open* affect programs . . . that allow for learning to affect both what activates the program (input) and what responses the program brings about (output)" (2018, p. 78). Denying first that basic emotions require a one-to-one correspondence between particular emotions and particular responses, and then that particular instances of the same basic emotion require a coordinated response, Scarantino suggests that a newly conceived BET can address the perennial objections of constructivists. What's more, this new BET importantly sees basic emotions as not aligning with folk psychological emotion categories, but rather as reflecting "theoretically motivated subcategories such as *unconditioned basic fear, conditioned basic fear, body-boundary violation basic disgust, core ingestive basic disgust, defensive basic anger*, and so forth" (2015, p. 363); the emphasis is on motive states, and flexibility of response (2018).

As already suggested, another modern expansion of basic/discrete emotion theory can be seen in the recent research of Cowen, Keltner, and colleagues. Their foundational work found that the evaluation of 2,185 short video clips resulted in "27+ linearly separable dimensions of reported emotion experience" (Cowen & Keltner, 2018, p. 275), dimensions that are "represented within a semantic space best captured by categorical [emotion] labels" – but the "boundaries between categories of emotion are fuzzy rather than discrete," meaning that "many categories of emotional experience share smooth gradients with other semantically distinct categories, forming smooth transitions between particular varieties of reported emotional experience" (Cowen & Keltner, 2017, pp. E7900, E7903). Functional magnetic resonance imaging (fMRI) analysis equally showed evidence for these more than twenty-seven distinct emotion categories, finding that "neural representations of diverse emotional experiences during video viewing are high-dimensional, categorical, and distributed across transmodal brain regions"; furthermore, "ratings of individual emotions could accurately be predicted from activity patterns in many brain regions, revealing that distributed brain networks contributed in distinct ways to the representation of individual emotions in a highly consistent manner across subjects" (Horikawa et al., 2020, pp. 14, 13). Subsequent studies found evidence for twenty-four distinct kinds of emotional experience in vocal bursts (Cowen, Elfenbein, et al., 2019), and twenty-eight emotions evident in naturalistic expression (Cowen & Keltner, 2020; see also Cowen et al., 2021).

Such "high-dimensional taxonomy of emotion" (Cowen, Sauter, et al., 2019, p. 85) led to the development of *semantic space theory*, a computational approach suggesting "upwards of 25 distinct kinds of emotions, each with their own patterned profile of associated responses" (Cowen & Keltner, 2021, p. 132). Contrary to the position of constructivists, this model holds that distinct categorical labels better account for emotional experience than a small number of dimensions like *arousal* and *valence* – indeed, in this high-dimensional approach, "dimensions of semantic spaces of emotion most typically correspond to individual emotions" (Keltner, Brooks, & Cowen, 2023, p. 243) – but at the same time, it distances itself from traditional categorical methods of BET, arguing that the fuzziness of boundaries renders individual emotions *distinct* but not *discrete*. Still, as we have seen, Keltner, Sauter, et al. (2019) and Keltner, Tracy, et al. (2019) nonetheless argue for the viability of a modern, revised basic emotion theory, and his semantic space model can in some ways be seen as an example of it, in the sense that it uses new analytical techniques to conclude that "21 emotions meet Ekman's criteria for 'basic' emotions, being associated with distinct antecedents, experiences, expressions, and neurophysiological correlates" (Keltner, Brooks, & Cowen, 2023, p. 245). A recent study (Floman et al., 2023) also found that participants reliably matched core relational themes (Lazarus, 1991) to twenty-four distinct emotions, providing evidence for semantic space theory and the foundational, universal nature of its emotional dimensions.

## Defining Universality

The universality question, then, is far from settled. This is particularly apparent when we also consider the fact that the very notion of "universality" is itself a more flexible and fluid designation than is often thought. For good reason, the matter of universality is often understood (particularly by anti-universalists) to reflect a rigid, absolute binary. But as Russell and Fernández-Dols (1997) noted long ago, when speaking of universality we need not be beholden to "the presupposition that we face an either-or choice: either randomness . . . or full universality" (p. 16) – that is, somewhat surprisingly, there are actually many different kinds of universality, which makes the universality of emotion a more complex and more potentially plausible proposition.

In the context of facial expression research, Russell and Fernández-Dols thus proposed the notion of *minimum universality*, which "predicts a certain amount of cross-cultural similarity in interpreting facial expressions without postulating an innate emotion signaling system"; the designation *minimal*, in this formulation, is "meant to emphasize that at least this much universality appears to exist" (1997, p. 16). Other options also exist. In linguistics, for example, it is perfectly normal to differentiate between "two senses of 'universal': the absolute (exceptionless) and the statistical (tendency-based) universal" (Bickel, 2014, p. 110). While these concepts have a technically precise usage in the context of language science, Hogan (2003) has fruitfully employed them outside of linguistics in his exploration of literary (and more generally, human) universals, demonstrating that universality need not *only* refer to things that occur in all instances without exception (i.e. *absolute* universals) but can also reflect things that occur in populations significantly more than we would expect by chance alone (i.e. *statistical* universals). Speaking of emotional expression, for example, Lee and Anderson (2016) note that there are some general patterns of cross-cultural consistency – in the sense that "if our expressions were purely higher-order associations, each shaped arbitrarily for social communication, there could not be any recognition of expressions across cultures" – which means that "basic expressions need not be universal in the strong sense but in having maintained statistical stability across the myriad of influences of culture and context they would indicate a common ancestry" (p. 497). Other scholars have similarly made distinctions between different types of human universals, such as Lonner's (1980) seven-level structure or Brown's (2001) five-plus categories. On a different note, in anthropology the notion of *contingent universals* refers to the shaping rules and principles that govern a particular cultural context (Harré & Llored, 2018; Shweder, 1991). And in terms of psychological universality, Norenzayan and Heine (2005) differentiate between four levels, reflecting how various cultures employ cognitive tools: they posit "nonuniversals (different tools), existential universals (same tool but differential functions), functional universals (same tool and same function or use but differential accessibilities), and accessibility universals (same tool, use, and degree of accessibility)" (p. 772). Manokara and Sauter (forthcoming) have recently used these criteria to consider existing evidence about emotion, finding different degrees of universality at different levels of analysis. In terms of emotion, it seems clear that the general concept of universality must not be seen as an *absolute/absent* binary, as there are many *different* ways that emotions may be thought (or not thought) to be meaningfully "universal."

Another common confusion regarding emotional universality entails the assumption that advocating for universal emotions inherently entails arguing for biological innateness. While it is certainly true that many theorists believe that universal aspects of emotion are "hardwired" into human biology – and many constructivists argue that the lack of discernible biological "signatures" proves that emotions are not universal – it is perfectly possible that some aspects of human emotion might be meaningfully universal but not biologically innate. As Hogan (2008a) notes, human universals (including universals of emotion) might arise "from regularities in the physical environment, recurring developmental experiences that are not genetically programmed, emergent features of the phenomenology of self-consciousness, convergent results of group dynamics, network patterns, etc." (p. 203). Similarly, Camras, Fatani, Fraumeni, and Shuster (2016) observe that "what are often considered to be universal discrete emotions" may actually reflect "universal environmental circumstances," in the sense that the apparent "innateness" of emotion may lie "in the universality of environmental 'control parameters' that engender the organization of responses as much as in the sets of responses themselves" (pp. 262–263). Clore (2018) suggests that "there may be more 'basicness' and 'universality' in … schemas and scripts about emotions than in emotions themselves" (p. 189). Power and Dalgleish (2015) write that the apparent universality of certain "basic" emotions might reflect that "there are a number of common and central appraisal scenarios, distinct from each other, which emerge in human societies and which underlie and shape emotional development," even if "the existence and development of these appraisal scenarios will differ somewhat across cultures" (p. 66). And Majeed (2023), taking a discrete approach, advocates for "a new version of faculty psychology that takes emotions to be products of developmental modules: non-innate systems which behave like modules, but form on the basis of various ontogenetic processes" (p. 1439). These possibilities are all at least plausible, so it seems clear that the truth of human emotional universality will not hinge on the proving or disproving of innate, biologically affective signatures.

It is also important to note that investigations into the universality of emotion are naturally complicated by the fact that when scholars consider emotion, they are often examining very different things. Beatty (2019) reminds us that even the question of what emotions are "depends on what level of analysis you are using, what order of reality you are describing" (p. 18), and this has obvious implications for any assessment of emotional universality. We find this generally acknowledged in an exchange between neuroscientist Jaak Panksepp and psychologist James A. Russell concerning categorical versus dimensional models of affect: Panksepp (2012) notes that "one key point of consilience" might be found in the fact that "Jim's empirical work proceeds completely at the tertiary-process level of psychological analysis, and mine largely at the primary process level" (pp. 313, 317). Decades ago, Mesquita and Frijda (1992) recognized that "whether cross-cultural differences or similarities are found depends to an important degree on the level of description of emotional phenomenon" (p. 179); recent cross-cultural analysis of emotional expression suggests that while display rules vary in different cultural contexts, there are certain stable underlying principles, such as "a universal norm for the management of emotional expressions" and a universal "display rule norm for greater expressivity toward ingroups than toward outgroups" (Hwang & Matsumoto, 2020, p. 260). Furthermore, Manokara and Sauter (forthcoming) crucially argue that "the question of whether emotions are universal or not must consider different components of emotions separately, and should recognise the possibility that the answers may not be consistent across components" – in other words, "the degree to which cross-cultural similarities and differences are observed may depend on which component of that emotion is being examined," and thus "universality for different components of emotions can be most usefully understood within a framework that differentiates between different *degrees* of universality" (p. 2).

What's more, the "psychological construct of a universal human nature," Lewis, Al-Shawaf, Conroy-Beam, Asao, and Buss (2017) note, "refers to species-typical *psychological mechanisms*, not universal *manifest behavior*" (p. 366), so it is quite obvious that the question of whether all human beings share universal emotion *potentials* cannot simply be answered by pointing to the obvious fact that all human cultures exhibit different emotional *practices* (see Mesquita, 2001). This leads Smaldino and Schank (2012) to observe that "the problem with identifying invariant emotional categories is complicated by the fact that people are adaptive systems, whose emotions are highly flexible," meaning that universal "invariants must therefore be sought in the mechanisms that allow them to produce these feelings, [the] mechanisms of affective responses" (p. 164) – and indeed, it has long been recognized that "constructionists have tended to focus on the *management* of emotions, in response to emotion norms; and positivists, on their *production*" (MacKinnon, 1994, p. 126). Finally, it may also simply be the case that certain emotions are more universal than others. For example, some scholars argue that core *primary* emotions – evolutionarily basic, largely hardwired responses to adaptive challenges – mix together to form more culturally elaborated *secondary* (or even *tertiary*) emotions (Kemper, 1987; Plutchik, 1980, 2003; J. H. Turner, 2000, 2021). These sentiments still have a biological basis, and may be part of a universal psychic architecture, but they are shaped much more specifically by social forces: Turner and Stets (2005), for example, suggest that "the most reasonable conclusion is that the expression of primary emotions is hardwired and universal, and that the capacity for first- and second-order emotions is also wired into the human neuroanatomy, with the gestural expression of these emotions determined by socialization into the emotion culture of a society" (pp. 19–20).

## Hybrid Models

Thus, there are many ways to think about emotional universality in a more nuanced manner than is sometimes assumed – and, even more importantly, such nuances allow for potential reconciliation with anti-universalist positions. As the first two sections of this Element have indicated, there is undeniable evidence for both consistency and variance in cross-cultural human emotional experience, and for this reason scholars from many disciplines have become increasingly inclined to develop models of emotion that account for both similarities and differences. In the general realm of psychology, for example, some scholars like Colombetti have addressed the issue by using a *dynamic systems* approach, which views emotions "as complex dynamical patterns of brain and bodily events" (2013, p. 46; see also Colombetti, 2009); the model of Lewis & Liu (2011), for example, "integrates the nativist assumption of pre-specified neural structures underpinning basic emotions with the constructionist view that emotions are assembled from psychological constituents" (p. 416), while that of Cunningham, Dunfield, and Stillman (2013) aims at "not only understanding the homogeneity of emotional experience (the similarities among instances of 'fear'), but also the heterogeneity of emotional experiences (the differences among the 'fear' episodes" (p. 353). Most recently, in fact, Wood and Coan (2023) have explicitly argued that a dynamic systems approach can reconcile the seeming opposition of basic/discrete emotion theories and con-structivist theories on the matter of universality: they propose that "at the level of goal-directed behavior, emotions are relatively universal, discrete, and adap-tive – one might say *evolved* – but also *necessarily* constructed through the body's interaction with the environment" (p. 443). There is also the network *psychometric model* of Lange, Dalege, Borsboom, van Kleef, and Fischer (2020; see also Lange & Zickfeld, 2021), in which "emotions are conceptual-ized as systems of causally interacting emotion components"; attempting to unite the major strands of modern emotion theory, this approach allows for "(a) identifying distinct emotions (central in affect-program theories), (b) between- and within-person variations of emotions (central in constructionist theories), and (c) causal relationships between emotion components (central in appraisal theories)" (p. 444). Other approaches invite us to reframe our very understanding of seemingly firm concepts like "construction." Acknowledging the seemingly indisputable evidence that *some* aspects of emotion are con-structed, Parkinson (2012) nonetheless moves beyond traditional models of social construction, exploring instead how "a set of processes whereby inter-personal, institutional, and cultural factors make their mark as emotions are put together over time"; crucially, in this account "no absolutist claim that all emotions are fully constituted by these processes is intended" (p. 291).

Beyond psychology, compromise positions are becoming increasingly important in other disciplines. In sociology, Ariza (2021) writes, "the need has been identified for the sociology of emotions to add complexity to its formulations of perception and experience by incorporating their biological correlates, without neglecting the social and phenomenological aspects" (p. 168); Bericat (2016) argues that the field needs "a greater degree of interaction between theory and empirical research, structural and cultural approaches and micro- and macro-perspectives" (p. 505). To this end, Demertzis (2020) adopts an "intermediate approach of mild constructionism," reflecting that "basic emotions provide a minimum of affective-cultural universals, a thin foundation whereby an infinite array of situationally formed emotions flourish" (p. 44). Similarly, J. H. Turner (2021) believes that "we do not have to take a firm stand on the essentialist and constructivist arguments for the nature of emotions," when we acknowledge that "many emotions . . . are biology based, with this base being expanded by reflexive thinking about emotions, by collective and self-discourse about emotions, and by codification of various beliefs and normative views on emotions that are part of a population's and various subpopulations' culture" (p. 177).

In 1996, Leavitt noted that "anthropology is divided between views of the emotions as primarily biological and as primarily sociocultural in nature" – but just as he then proposed "ways around the meaning/feeling dichotomy," so too have other, more recent anthropologists adopted a more hybrid position (p. 514). Such approaches note that emotions must "be thought of as both biological and cultural, as consisting of both physical feeling and cultural meaning" (Milton, 2005, p. 198). Quinn and Mathews (2016), for example, suggest that "the highly variable selves that ethnographers have documented cross-culturally all build upon the universal human self described by neuro-biologists"; for them, "the link between cultural selfhood and this neurally-based self is emotional arousal" (p. 359). Stodulka (2017) notes that while "feelings are related to biographical, social, politics, and cultural dimensions," a "too skeptical Geertzian rhetoric that rejects the universal biological dimension of emotion-related phenomena and withdraws to a constructivist phenomenology obstructs anthropology's epistemological resourcefulness" (pp. 14, 11). His "integrative anthropology of emotion" thus sees affects as "bio-cultural processes [that] relate physiological arousals and their cognitive appraisals with their surrounding local worlds in terms of a mutually shared cultural rhetoric" (p. 15).

More elaborately, Beatty (2019) considers "emotion in its different guises and from different perspectives," in "recognition of the diversity of emotion in

form, context, and use"; accordingly, he does "not come down decisively for or
against a natural kind view of emotion, or even for or against the coherence of
the emotion concept," but rather takes a "strategic scepticism [that allows him]
to open things up, recovering some of the essential detail of person, history, and
circumstance that has been lost in reductive approaches" (p. 12). Accordingly,
he develops a "narrative approach" that "does not depend on a view of emotions
as discrete biological events governed by mechanisms that evolved to deal with
threats and opportunities, [but] nor does it embrace an out-and-out cultural
relativism" (p. 17). His outlook – which anchors both the apprehension and
reporting of emotion within a complex account of emotion's core narrativity –
thus affirms "a multiplex reality [that] salvages the bridge to cross-cultural
understanding that relativism would sweep away," but that "also avoids the
empiricist limitations of basic emotions theories that tend to ignore all that
concerns the anthropologist – motives, plans, meaning, the social drama"
(p. 19). When describing, for example, an anthropological event like a funeral
scene, he rightly notes that "pan-human, culturally specific, [and] idiosyncratic"
factors are all at play (p. 193); in this, he follows Nussbaum (2001), who notes
that "all human emotions . . . bear traces of a history that is at once commonly
human, socially constructed, and idiosyncratic" (p. 177).

   In linguistics, we have seen how certain *primary* metaphors seem to consistently reflect universal cognitive architecture, but Winter and Matlock
(2017) remind that this doesn't mean that such metaphors are simply *acul-
tural*; they suggest that "linguistic and cultural reflections of primary metaphors may thus 'feed back' into the underlying conceptual structure," leading
to the conclusion that "primary metaphors are both cultural and embodied"
(p. 100). For example, the cognitive linguist Kövecses (2000a) argues that the
evidence of language use points to a "body-based social constructionism,"
a view that sees emotions like anger as "both (near) universal and culture-
specific," in the sense that they reflect "universal elements of the body (human
physiology) and culture-specific elements of cultural explanation (of different
kinds)" (p. 169; see also Kövecses 2000b). Perovíc and Vuković-Stanatović
(2021) have more recently found that the "level of universality and culture-
specificity depends on how generally we define the conceptualization" of the
metaphor – their analysis of *love* metaphor, metonymy, and cultural scripts
suggests that "more general and abstract metaphors displayed more universality [i.e. metaphors at the *superordinate-level*], whereas more cultural specificity was likely to be found in the basic-level metaphors, i.e. narrower
metaphors" (p. 45).

   Finally, we saw in Section 2 how historians tend to be vehement opponents of
universalism, and even those that incorporate the empirical sciences into their

approach will often still reject the notion that any aspect of emotion is meaningfully universal. There are, however, some exceptions. Reddy, we saw, attacked basic emotion theory (2020), but his entry into the field (1997) was entitled "Against Constructionism"; more notably, his most enduring work, *The Navigation of Feeling* (2001), elaborates a "formal theory that establishes emotions as largely (but not entirely) learned," a model that "leaves plenty of room for cultural variation" but also posits "a core concept of emotions, universally applicable, that allows one to say what suffering is, and why we all deserve to live in freedom" (p. xi). More recently, Dixon (2020) – who, we saw, also attacked universalizing discourses – notes that one might oppose basic emotion theory in its narrowest conception while still acknowledging that there may be "some physiologically grounded dimensions to ... emotion-like experiences in all cultures" (p. 29). But perhaps the most promising compromise model is that of Firth-Godbehere (2021), who uses the mechanics of disgust to exemplify "the way emotions can be understood from both the universalist and constructivist standpoints": it "could easily be the case," he writes, that "there's a basic evolved feeling designed to stop us from poisoning ourselves and picking up parasites," which "is then adapted, shaped, and manipulated by culture" (p. 259). In this way, it is perfectly possible for historians to be sensitive to the historical and cultural contingencies of emotion without denying that certain functional affective properties may be generally consistent across the species.

## The Biocultural View

Beyond such specific disciplinary approaches, scholars are increasingly acknowledging that our analysis of emotion should be more cross-disciplinary, and that we should attempt to bridge theoretical boundaries by drawing on the insights of both traditionally universalist and traditionally anti-universalist disciplines. Indeed, Tappolet (2023) has recently concluded that "neither the arguments for biological determinism nor the ones for social constructionism are convincing," because it is more "plausible that emotions are instead seamless products of the interaction of nature and culture" (pp. 39, 55).

In the study of emotion and beyond, an increasing number of scholars (like, we saw above, Stodulka) are thus embracing some sort of *biocultural* approach, which J. Carroll et al. (2018) define as an "integrative research program designed to investigate the causal interactions between biological adaptations and cultural constructions": that is, it posits that "cultural processes are rooted in the biological necessities of the human life cycle," while "human biological processes are constrained, organized, and developed by culture" (p. 1). One must be slightly wary with terminology, because in some places (particularly in humanist spaces) *biocultural* implies less of a synthesis between universalist and constructivists positions than one might suspect; for these scholars, J. Carroll (2022b) notes: "the biological part of the biocultural model is only the domain-general brain that enables culture," meaning that they use the term *biocultural* to account for an outlook that is, in practice, almost entirely constructivist (p. 83). But there are plenty of more conciliatory instances. Such versions of a biocultural outlook are premised on *culture-gene coevolutionary theory*, which posits that "cultural and genetic selection both affect how the mind and brain give rise to behavior" (Chiao & Immordino-Yang, 2013, p. 57; see Boyd & Richerson, 1985); indeed, decades ago, Nesse (1990) noted that "debates about whether traits result from nature or nurture" will increasingly "become less simplistic as more people realize that all phenotypes represent the outcome of genotypes interacting with environments" (p. 279).

Accordingly, scholars now focus on "the feedback loops between genetic evolution and cultural practices across the course of human and prehuman evolution" (J. Carroll et al., 2018, p. 3), and biological reductionism is avoided by acknowledging that "cultural evolution affects biological evolution, and that cultural practices can exert pressure on the human genome," in the sense that "physical, but also material, historical, social and cultural environments in which we live, and even the type of human relations characterizing our life, all influence the expression of our genes" (Wojciehowski & Gallese, 2018, 10). Sauter and Russell (2024) elaborate:

> Rather than simply operating as two forces opposing each other, biological and cultural factors *interact*. Such interactions open the door to exciting research. Some genes vary between populations and can affect culture via psychological predispositions to cultural learning by, for example, biasing transmission of information towards some cultural variants of a behavior over others[.] On the other hand, cultural practices can also affect a group's gene pool; a well-known example is the low prevalence of the genotype for lactose intolerance in cultural groups that have historically kept dairy cattle. (p. 551)

"In short," they conclude, "over time, changes in culture can lead to genetic changes; and genetic differences can influence culture." At the level of individuals, an increased understanding of the brain's *neuroplasticity* similarly attests to the viability of a biocultural approach (Rubin, 2009). Reconciling universalist and constructivist approaches, the biocultural outlook thus allows us to imagine a model of the mind in which emotional mechanisms "do not start out as empty shells, devoid of information" – certain "circuits are already there, unfolding over development, influenced but not totally constructed by experience" (Ekman & Cordaro, 2011, p. 367). Or, as Jonsson (2021) succinctly puts it, "human emotions are flexible within constraints" (p. 28).

Mason and Capitanio (2012), for example, reconfigure the concept of basic emotions within terms of epigenetic development:

> From a developmental systems perspective, basic emotions are not innate. They are not illusory. Nor are they created by the forces of culture or custom. Instead it seems more likely that what are usually construed as basic emotions are they outcome of a natural developmental process that depends on an appropriate enabling environment (e.g. an environment of evolutionary adaptedness), and the proper genome interacting in ways that are "customary" based on the evolutionary history of the species. (p. 243)

Buck (2014) similarly theorizes a *developmental-interactionist* outlook, which he terms a "general biosocial approach that views emotions in terms of emergent systems involving an interaction between biological potential and social experience over the course of development" (p. xx). Recent *social functionalist theory* (Keltner et al., 2022) equally considers "the bidirectional influences between culture, relationship, and emotion" (p. 388); a model that "extend[s] Basic Emotion Theory," it focuses on how discrete emotions organize around human social relational needs, but still acknowledges that "culture shapes emotion in profound ways, in the beliefs, practices, rituals, ceremonies, and institutions that shape the contexts, appraisals, and forms of conceptualization that imbue emotion with culturally specific meaning" (pp. 389, 395; see also Keltner, Haidt, & Shiota, 2006). Similarly, some recent work on emotion in cross-cultural psychology now explicitly frames itself in biocultural terms, with goals of "integrating biological universality with cultural specificity"; this model posits "a biologically based core emotion system that is calibrated, regulated, and elaborated by culture," and acknowledges that "different domains of emotion are more relatively influenced by biology or culture" (Matsumoto & Hwang, 2019, pp. 361, 398; Matsumoto & Hwang, 2012, p. 91). Kamiloğlu, Cong, Sun, and Sauter (2024) vitally note that "evolved mechanisms do not imply strict uniformity," and thus argue that "evolved psychological mechanisms result in cultural differences instantiated as variations around common themes of human universals" (p. 983). And Watzl (2019) goes even further, suggesting that "social mechanisms may be so deeply intertwined with other biological mechanism that it makes no sense to ask about their relative contributions" (p. 46). It seems clear that, as Boddice (2024) has recently put it, "there is no culture-free or value-neutral context to the study of human 'nature,' and there is no 'nurture' without framed biology" (p. 13).

A particularly valuable biocultural account of the complex entanglement of emotional regularity and emotional variance may be found in the ongoing efforts of researchers working under the umbrella of *cultural neuroscience* (Chiao, 2009, 2015, 2018; Chiao & Immordino-Yang, 2013; Chiao et al., 2016; Han, 2017; Han et al., 2013), a relatively new, multidisciplinary approach that draws from fields such as cultural psychology, anthropology, and cognitive science. Put simply, cultural neuroscience "examines how cultural and bio-logical mechanisms *mutually* shape human behavior across phylogenetic, development, and situational timescales" (Chiao, 2015, p. 282; emphasis added); it is thus premised on culture-gene coevolutionary theory. Because of its linkage to cultural psychology, much work in cultural neuroscience is concerned with investigating the "neural substrates of cultural diversity of human cognition and emotion" and how "individuals from different socio-cultural contexts show distinct patterns of brain activity in cognition and behavior" (Han et al., 2013, pp. 337, 338). Yet, at the same time, the field equally recognizes "a hierarchy of neural universals within levels of the nervous system," including "neural states, ranging from molecules to systems, that are ... observable to people of all cultures," "neural states that have the same function or are physically implemented for the same purpose across situations or cultural contexts," and "neural states that are implemented with the same degree of ease and frequency across cultural contexts" (Chiao, 2018, p. 35). As such, the final goal of cultural neuroscience is to "unveil both culturally universal and culturally unique neural processes" (Han, 2017, p. 22), and researchers are indeed "discovering both generalizable and culturally specific mechanisms of the mind, brain, and behavior" (Chiao et al., 2016, p. xix).

Cultural neuroscience shows a particular interest in the working of emotion, and research has already demonstrated how "cultural meaning-making shapes the biological correlates of emotional feelings" (Immordino-Yang & Yang, 2017, p. 34) and how the brain's construction of emotion is "at least partly open to cultural influence" (Immordino-Yang, Yang, & Damasio, 2014, p. 1). But most exciting is how the field promises to synthesize various insights from the major (competing) models of emotion that we have examined in the previ-ous two sections. According to Chiao (2015), cultural neuroscience helps us realize that "the four classical theories of emotion (e.g. basic emotion, cognitive appraisal, psychological construction, and social construction) are all, to a certain degree, simultaneously correct," in the sense that each explores "processes of emotion generation and experience, but each at a different level of analysis, and all of which are important and necessary for adaptive emotional behavior to occur" (p. 281). Cultural neuroscience thus provides an overarching framework for attending to both "the dual processes of genetic and cultural inheritance" – the domain of BET and social constructionism – and "the refinement of cognitive and neural architecture that accompanies genetic and cultural selection of human emotional behavior" – the domain of appraisal theory and psychological constructionism. For this reason, it is an especially promising methodology for moving beyond the simplistic opposition of emotional universality and emotional variance. A vaguely related approach with a somewhat different focus has been called *cross-cultural affective neuroscience* (CAN): emerging from the work of Panksepp, it studies the "two-way interaction between self and culture," in terms of how "(1) universally shared subcortical affective systems are initially regulated uniquely in each mother-infant bond and subsequently by family models and cultures and (2) culture, by effecting family models and mothering styles, influences the degree to which subcortical basic affective systems are reinforced or inhibited" (Özkarar-Gradwohl, 2019, p. 4).

## Underlying Structure

Biocultural approaches thus have great potential to account for both patterns of emotional consistency and emotional variance, in a way that complicates any easy distinction between universalist and anti-universalist perspectives. The existence of variance within a universal framework might also be clarified if we turn to approaches positing that emotional particularity emerges from some sort of underlying universal structure. For example, in the 1980s and 1990s, scholars in different fields took a *prototype* perspective, which generally posited that cross-culturally ubiquitous prototype models of emotions lie behind cultural particularity (Fehr, 1988, 1994, 2005; Fehr & Russell, 1984, 1991; Lakoff & Kövecses, 1987; Russell & Fehr, 1994; Shaver, Wu, & Schwartz, 1992; Shaver et al., 1987).

Parrott (2010, 2012) and Frijda and Parrott's (2011) more recent concept of *ur-emotions* is a particularly helpful, prototype-like model that identifies a structure underpinning emotional variance. Proposing that we move away from the concept of basic emotions, Parrott introduces the idea of *ur-emotion*, which "refers to the structure or archetype that underlies an emotion that is evolutionarily related and recognizably shared between cultures and species, but [is] not identical to the occurring emotion itself" (2010, p. 20). According to this theory, "it is not multicomponential response patterns [of emotion] that are universal ... but rather something more abstract"; ur-emotions are thus "the core element in multicomponential response patterns" (Frijda & Parrott, 2011, pp. 406, 407), in the sense that they are "an aspect of actual emotional states, but are not themselves actual, occurring emotions" (Parrott, 2010, p. 20). These core elements, more specifically, are "motive states or states of action readiness" that "specify particular motivational, motor, and cognitive response processes" – that is, they reflect certain universally available human response patterns, such as *affiliate* ("achieving or accepting close interpersonal interaction"), *reject* ("refusing interaction"), and *desire* ("achieving positive hedonic outcome") (Frijda & Parrott, 2011, pp. 406, 408, 409). (These tendencies are similar to Lazarus's [1991] notion of *core relational themes.*) The great value of this approach is that "ur-emotions can be perceived in similar but nonidentical emotions in different cultures or species"; so, for example, "when comparing the anger of the British to that of the Utku Eskimos or Yanamamo native South Americans, *ur-emotion* suggests the similarity without suggesting that the vast differences in socialization, evaluation, social norms, cultural centrality, and social consequences have no effect on the emotion's form, function, or subjective experience" (Parrott, 2010, pp. 20, 18). Parrott elaborates:

> Consider, for example, that there are many differences between the emotions *marah* (in Indonesian), *ikari* (in Japanese), *song* (in Ifaluk), and *anger* (in English), but in all of them the ur-emotion of *antagonism* is evident – all four are aimed at an object that is appraised as interfering in some way with one's concerns, and all four give rise to a motivation to stop that interference in different, culturally appropriate ways. (Parrott, 2012, p. 248)

The theory of ur-emotions, then, explains how the universal motivational state of *submission* can variously form the basis of culturally inflected emotional experiences such as *shame*, *awe*, *admiration*, *humility*, or *respect*, depending on how the event is appraised and what additional affective components build upon the core. It also explains how the culturally particular sentiment *amae* – a word in Japanese referring to the pleasurable abandonment of oneself to a caregiver, and an emotion usually said to be nonnative to the affective repertoire of Anglo-Americans – still emerges from the cross-culturally universal position of *submission* (Frijda & Parrott, 2011, p. 411). This, it seems to me, is a quite sensible way to account for the fact that emotions are culturally constructed from universal human potentials.

From the perspective of linguistics, universal structure is also featured in the theory of Natural Semantic Metalanguage (NSM), a model that similarly tends to both emotional universality and cultural particularity (Harkins & Wierzbicka, 2001; Wierzbicka, 1986, 1992, 1996, 1998, 1999, 2009; for overviews see Durst, 2003; Goddard, 2021). Like Ortony, Clore, and Collins's (1988) attempt to "specify, in as language-neutral a manner as possible, the characteristics of distinct emotions" (p. 9), NSM works by "establishing lists of semantic primitives that exist in all languages and that could allow differentiation between synonyms or their translation equivalents" (Santos & Maia, 2018, p. 5):

> The Natural Semantic Metalanguage (NSM) approach is a cognitive approach to meaning which uses a metalanguage of simple, cross-translatable words as its principal method of representation. At base, this metalanguage relies on 65 semantic/conceptual primes (often termed simply, semantic primes), for example: I and YOU, SOMEONE and SOMETHING, HAPPEN and DO, WANT and KNOW, GOOD and BAD, IF and BECAUSE. Semantic primes are posited to be shared human concepts, and evidence suggests that they manifest themselves as words or word- like expressions in all or most human languages. (Goddard, 2021, p. 93)

Different feelings are conceptualized as sets of clauses within the metalanguage, meaning that "there is an almost infinite set of possibilities for emotions to be lexicalized in different societies, while at the same time, every emotion can be translated and therefore understood by every human being" (Santos & Maia, 2018, p. 5). Most crucially, Wierzbicka argues that English psychological terms like *anger* and *sadness* are distinctly not universal, but they nonetheless can be distilled into scripts reflecting the universal meta-language, which allows us "to explore human emotions from a culture-independent perspective": we can do this, she argues, "when we stop trying to describe other people's emotions through English terms such as *anger*, *sadness* and *fear* (or even through their 'scientific' versions such as 'affect program anger,' 'affect program sadness' and 'affect program fear') and try to understand them instead through the conceptual vocabulary shared by speakers of all languages, that is, through universal human concepts" (2009, pp. 3, 13; see also Wierzbicka, 2014). Although NSM has been subject to criticism (Matthewson, 2003; Riemer, 2006), the methodology has nonetheless been fruitfully used to examine a variety of emotion concepts (Gladkova, Vanhatalo, & Goddard, 2016; Goddard, 2014, 2015; Ye, 2001).

A final valuable prototype-like approach can be found within a particular strand of appraisal theory. It will be remembered from Section 1 that certain appraisal theories posit that the human appraisal mechanism gives rise to discrete, essentially universal emotions; other appraisal theories, however, split "emotional episodes into a large or even infinite number of subsets, each characterized by a unique situation and hence a unique pattern of appraisal values" (Moors, 2014, p. 303). Scherer's (1984, 2001, 2009b) *component process model* belongs to this second category. This model sits somewhere between the extreme poles of basic emotion theory and constructivism; it proposes that "research move from a discrete emotion approach to an emotion process approach," but also states that while it is true that "individuals construct their own categorization of experience and choose an emotion label accordingly" (i.e. the psychological construction outlook), it is also "essential to theoretically link this act to what precedes it in the emotion process, allowing at least some degree of prediction" (Scherer & Moors, 2019, pp. 738, 739).

In Scherer's theory, humans respond to stimuli in light of several appraisal objectives, evaluating the events via a "subjective assessment ... of consequences and implications on a background of personal needs, goals, and values" (2009b, p. 1309); consequently, emotions are dynamic processes that emerge when such multilevel appraisals give rise to things like *physiological response patterns, motivational changes*, and *categorization/verbal labeling.* While Scherer may see universality in the appraisal mechanism (1997), he distinctly does *not* see emotional experiences themselves as universal; the component process model "does not assume the existence of a limited set of discrete emotions or affect programmes," but instead, because there is no limit to the number of ways that events could be subjectively appraised by an organism, "considers the possibility of an infinite number of different types of emotion episode[s]" (2009b, p. 1316).

But even as it acknowledges the boundless nature of emotion, the component process model still accounts for patterns of emotional regularity, via the concept of *modal emotions* (Scherer, 1994, 2009a). Scherer notes that in the course of normal human existence, "some combinations [of appraisals]" have tended "to occur more frequently than others as part of an emotional reaction," probably "due to general conditions of life, constraints of social organisation, and similarity of innate equipment" that the species possesses; there are therefore "some major patterns of adaptation [in] life ... that reflect frequently recurring patterns of environmental evaluation results" (1994, pp. 25, 28; 2009b, p. 1316). He uses the name *modal emotions* to account for such prototypical "patterning of expression, autonomic arousal, action tendencies, and feeling states" that arise from the "prototypical pattern[s] of appraisal" elicited by common life conditions in the species (1994, p. 30). Given "the prominence and frequency of occurrence of these episodes of highly similar emotional experiences, it is not surprising that they have been labeled with a short verbal expression, mostly a single word, in most languages"; for this reason, the subjective experience designated by the English word *frustration* (for example) is in effect "universal and ubiquitous," in the sense that "all organisms, at all stages of ontogenetic development, encounter blocks to need satisfaction or goal achievement at least some of the time" (p. 28).

Crucially, with the theory of modal emotions, "no effort is made to find or define a definite number or homogenous, integral categories or mechanisms that justify an a priori definition of basic or fundamental" – instead, what's acknowledged is the fact that certain prototypical appraisal patterns give rise to emotional episodes prototypically similar enough to have warranted inclusion in a broad linguistic or conceptual category (p. 30). Rather than positing discrete emotions or affect programs, the model thus postulates "fuzzy sets of modal emotions (as a result of a categorisation of qualia) on the background of an infinite variety of emotional processes and their qualia representations" (Scherer, 2009b, p. 1334). In this, it aligns with the suspicion of linguist Daneš (2004), who approached the universality versus cultural specificity of emotion debate by suggesting that "perhaps it would be [best] to use the metaphor of a field or space of fluctuating fuzzy elemental emotional states ... with relatively 'condensed islands,' more or less different in various cultures and identified by them by means of particular labels" (p. 31).

It has recently been argued (Boddice, 2024) that all attempts to find universal underpinnings of emotion – such as Parrott's ur-emotions, Wierzbicka's NSM, and Scherer's modal emotions – are inherently flawed, because they are bound to particular-language constructs. I find this position unconvincing, as it is premised on a linguistic relativism that is not, in my mind, supported either by common sense or by existing evidence, which points to countless forms of cross-cultural similarity and ubiquity in emotional language and emotional experience that cannot occur by chance alone. It is perfectly possible, for example, to find language-neutral ways to investigate whether "people of different cultures have similar subjective experiences when encountering equivalent situations" (Manokara & Sauter, forthcoming, p. 11), and it goes without saying that individuals are not emotionally bound by the linguistic repertoire of their native language. While it is absolutely true that the Ifaluk concept of *song* and the English concept of *anger* are not exactly equivalent, it seems odd to me that we should not be able to talk about their structural and functional similarities within their respective cultures, and prototype approaches are one way to do so that does not rely on an uncritical collapsing of the distinction between them.

## Concluding Thoughts

It seems likely that we are still far away from settling the "universality question." It is definitely possible, of course, that new affordances might allow future research to make empirical discoveries that will shed light on the issue; for example, technological advancement and improved research design may allow us, at some point in the future, to conclusively determine whether emotions have certain explicit "signatures" in the body (see Levenson, 2014). But until then, it is likely that researchers from across all disciplines will continue to amass evidence for both points of cross-cultural and cross-temporal affective contact and points of cross-cultural and cross-temporal affective divergence, and it will be the job of researchers to create models of emotion that account for both sets of findings. Given this, it may actually be valuable, at least rhetorically, to strategically exchange the concept of universality for one of ubiquity. As noted, universality is a poisoned term for many – especially humanists – and it may be too difficult to resuscitate for general scholarly usage, even if more technical applications (as we have also seen) entail a much less rigid concept than is often assumed. Speaking instead of emotional ubiquity – that is, emotional forms that recur in many, most, or ostensibly all contexts – may be more palatable to cross-disciplinary audiences. Saucier, Thalmayer, and Bel-Bahar (2014) offer a precise definition of observed ubiquity – "empirical occurrence in all members of a representative subset of all cultures," which in turn "means a high probability of universality" (p. 200). But even used more informally, ubiquity may be a helpful way to get at regularities that occur in the emotional lives of human populations, but one that does not discount the obvious fact of emotional variability.

Whatever the case, it seems that valuable advancements will come when researchers are increasingly inclined to consider whatever perspective on emotional universality is not common in their native discipline or theoretical framework. Ariza (2021), for example, recently notes:

> From a social science perspective, the need has been identified for the sociology of emotions to add complexity to its formulations of perception and experience by incorporating their biological correlates, without neglecting the social and phenomenological aspects. ... The social character of both processes – perception and experience – does not negate the central role of the somatosensory system of preferences, [but] it is equally necessary for neuroscience to refrain from considering society a mere externality of the individual organism that experiences emotions. (p. 168)

In other words, I think we will be best served the more that universalist theorists attempt to account for emotional variance in their models, and the more that anti-universalist theorists attempt to account for emotional regularity in their models. Because, most fundamentally, human universality and human difference are bound to one another. Long ago, Huntington and Metcalf

(1979) remarked that "cultural difference works on the universal human emotional material" (p. 43); more recently, Hogan (2008b) reflects that "there is no such thing as human culture or human cultural difference without human universality," in the sense that "cultural difference is variation on human universality" (p. 145). Roughley (2000) similarly wonders if "there aren't some concepts whose applicability to all humans needs to be assumed in order to even make sense of any version of the thesis of cultural relativism": if, for example,

> it is argued that the modern western self is structured in a way that is radically different from the forms taken on by the self for the ancient Greeks or members of contemporary non-western cultures, then it appears that there is some common entity which can be identified in the various cultures under scrutiny, in order to show how it differs in each case (p. 6).

Thus, it seems clear that we need to consider universality and difference in tandem.

In terms of emotional universality, I think the most sensible approach to the matter is encapsulated by Semin (2012): while acknowledging that emotions are by definition dynamic and constructed by socio-cultural contexts, he notes that "you can construct only by what your body, brain, and the social-physical conditions afford you to construct" (p. 230). That is, though human functioning (such as emotional experience) "finds different expressions in terms of the variable and evolving social environments they are part of and give rise to," this functioning is nonetheless still "constrained by relatively invariant ecological, existential, material, and biological conditions" – so, in the broadest sense, "our knowledge is advanced by understanding the balance between variation and systematicity." To this end, Matsumoto and Wilson (2022) have recently argued that "emotions represent an area of study that can be characterized by the simultaneous co-existence of both universality based on biological substrates and cultural differences based on learned constructions" (p. 926), and an increasing number of scholars are realizing this. Indeed, when reflecting on the content of their volume, the editors of *The Nature of Emotion: Fundamental Questions* (Fox et al., 2018) observed that "although the basic model and the constructivist model are often pitted against each other, most of the contributors . . . seem to acknowledge and, more importantly, make use of, both perspectives" (p. 404). As we move forward, this willingness to not only acknowledge but also attempt to reconcile universalist and anti-universalist positions will make us well positioned for the twenty-first-century study of emotion and beyond. I have surveyed many different disciplines in this Element, and the way that each field approaches such a reconciliation will undoubtedly be different – given that each varies in how it specifically understands matters of theory, evidence, and even "truth." But I think that all scholars are capable of building, rather than burning, theoretical bridges, and it seems clear that reading and thinking widely, with an aim to integrating various perspectives, will only serve to further elucidate the fascinating contours of human emotional experience.

# References

Abu-Lughod, L. (1986). *Veiled sentiments: Honor and poetry in a Bedouin society.* Berkeley: University of California Press.

Abu-Lughod, L., & Lutz, C. A. (1990). Introduction: Emotion, discourse, and the politics of everyday life. In C. A. Lutz, & L. Abu-Lughod (Eds.), *Language and the politics of emotion* (pp. 1–23). Cambridge: Cambridge University Press.

Adolphs, R. (2017). How should neuroscience study emotions? By distinguishing emotion states, concepts, and experiences. *Social Cognitive and Affective Neuroscience, 12*(1), 24–31.

Adolphs, R., & Anderson, D. J. (2018). *The neuroscience of emotion: A new synthesis.* Princeton: Princeton University Press.

Ahern, S. (2024). Affect theory and literary criticism. *Emotion Review, 16*(2), 96–106.

Ahmed, S. (2004). *The cultural politics of emotion.* Edinburgh: Edinburgh University Press.

Amberber, M. (2001). Testing emotional universals in Amharic. In J. Harkins, & A. Wierzbicka (Eds.), *Emotions in crosslinguistic perspective* (pp. 35–68). Berlin: De Gruyter.

Ariza, M. (2021). The sociology of emotions in Latin America. *Annual Review of Sociology, 47*(1), 157–175.

Armon-Jones, C. (1986a). The social functions of emotion. In R. Harré (Ed.), *The social construction of emotions* (pp. 57–82). Oxford: Basil Blackwell.

Armon-Jones, C. (1986b). The thesis of constructionism. In R. Harré (Ed.), *The social construction of emotions* (pp. 32–56). Oxford: Basil Blackwell.

Armony, J., & Vuilleumier, P. (Eds.). (2013). *The Cambridge handbook of human affective neuroscience.* Cambridge: Cambridge University Press.

Armstrong, P. B. (2020). *Stories and the brain: The neuroscience of narrative.* Baltimore: Johns Hopkins University Press.

Arnett, J. J. (2008). The neglected 95%: Why American psychology needs to become less American. *American Psychologist, 63*(7), 602–614.

Arnold, M. B. (1960). *Emotion and personality.* New York: Columbia University Press.

Asher, K. G. (2017). *Literature, ethics, and the emotions.* Cambridge: Cambridge University Press.

Auracher, J., Albers, S., Zhai, Y., Gareeva, G., & Stavniychuk, T. (2010). P is for happiness, N is for sadness: Universals in sound iconicity to detect emotions in poetry. *Discourse Processes, 48*(1), 1–25.

Averill, J. R. (1980). A constructivist view of emotion. In R. Plutchik, & H. Kellerman (Eds.), *Theories of emotion* (pp. 305–339). New York: Academic Press.

Averill, J. R. (1982). *Anger and aggression: An essay on emotion*. New York: Springer.

Averill, J. R. (1994). In the eyes of the beholder. In P. Ekman, & R. J. Davidson (Eds.), *The nature of emotion: Fundamental questions* (pp. 7–14). Oxford: Oxford University Press.

Averill, J. R. (2012). The future of social constructionism: Introduction to a special section of *Emotion Review*. *Emotion Review*, *4*(3), 215–220.

Aviezer, H., Hassin, R. R., Ryan, J., et al. (2008). Angry, disgusted, or afraid? Studies on the malleability of emotion perception. *Psychological Science*, *19* (7), 724–732.

Aviezer, H., Hassin, R. R., Bentin, S., & Trope, Y. (2008). Putting facial expressions back in context. In N. Ambady, & J. J. Skowronski (Eds.), *First impressions* (pp. 255–286). New York: Guilford.

Azari, B., Westlin, C., Satpute, A. B., et al. (2020). Comparing supervised and unsupervised approaches to emotion categorization in the human brain, body, and subjective experience. *Scientific Reports*, *10*(1), article 1.

Bamberg, M. (1997a). Emotion talk(s): The role of perspective in the construction of emotions. In S. Niemeier, & R. Dirven (Eds.), *The language of emotions* (pp. 209–225). Amsterdam: John Benjamins.

Bamberg, M. (1997b). Language, concepts and emotions: The role of language in the construction of emotions. *Language Sciences*, *19*(4), 309–340.

Barbalet, J. M. (1998). *Emotion, social theory, and social structure: A macrosociological approach*. Cambridge: Cambridge University Press.

Barclay, K. (2020). *The history of emotions: A student guide to methods and sources*. London: Bloomsbury.

Barclay, K. (2021a). Emotions in the history of emotions. *History of Psychology*, *24*(2), 112–115.

Barclay, K. (2021b). State of the field: The history of emotions. *History*, *106* (371), 456–466.

Barrett, L. F. (1998). Discrete emotions or dimensions? The role of valence focus and arousal focus. *Cognition and Emotion*, *12*(4), 579–599.

Barrett, L. F. (2006a). Are emotions natural kinds? *Perspectives on Psychological Science*, *1*(1), 28–58.

Barrett, L. F. (2006b). Solving the emotion paradox: Categorization and the experience of emotion. *Personality and Social Psychology Review*, *10*(1), 20–46.

Barrett, L. F. (2012). Emotions are real. *Emotion*, *12*(3), 413–429.

Barrett, L. F. (2013). Psychological construction: The Darwinian approach to the science of emotion. *Emotion Review, 5*(4), 379–389.

Barrett, L. F. (2017a). *How emotions are made: The secret life of the brain.* New York: Houghton Mifflin Harcourt.

Barrett, L. F. (2017b). The theory of constructed emotion: An active inference account of interoception and categorization. *Social Cognitive and Affective Neuroscience, 12*(1), 1–27.

Barrett, L. F. (2022). Context reconsidered: Complex signal ensembles, relational meaning, and population thinking in psychological science. *American Psychologist, 77*(8), 894–920.

Barrett, L. F., & Lida, T. (2024). Constructionist theories of emotion in psychology and neuroscience. In Scarantino, *Emotion theory*, pp. 350–387.

Barrett, L. F., & Russell, J. A. (1999). The structure of current affect: Controversies and emerging consensus. *Current Directions in Psychological Science, 8*(1), 10–14.

Barrett, L. F., & Satpute, A. B. (2019). Historical pitfalls and new directions in the neuroscience of emotion. *Neuroscience Letters, 693*, 9–18.

Barrett, L. F., Ochsner, K. N., & Gross, J. J. (2007). On the automaticity of emotion. In J. A. Bargh (Ed.), *Social psychology and the unconscious: The automaticity of higher mental processes* (pp. 173–217). New York: Psychology Press.

Barrett, L. F., Lindquist, K. A., Bliss-Moreau, E., et al. (2007). Of mice and men: Natural kinds of emotions in the mammalian brain? A response to Panksepp and Izard. *Perspectives on Psychological Science, 2*(3), 297–312.

Barrett, L. F., Mesquita, B., & Gendron, M. (2011). Context in emotion perception. *Current Directions in Psychological Science, 20*(5), 286–290.

Barrett, L. F., Wilson-Mendenhall, C. D., & Barsalou, L. W. (2015). The conceptual act theory: A roadmap. In L. F. Barrett, & J. A. Russell (Eds.), *The psychological construction of emotion* (pp. 83–110). New York: Guilford.

Barrett, L. F., Lewis, M., & Haviland-Jones, J. M. (Eds.). (2016). *Handbook of emotions: Fourth edition*. New York: Guilford.

Barrett, L. F., Adolphs, R., Marsella, S., Martinez, A. M., & Pollak, S. D. (2019). Emotional expressions reconsidered: Challenges to inferring emotion from human facial movements. *Psychological Science in the Public Interest, 20*(1), 1–68.

Bateson, G., & Mead, M. (1942). *Balinese character: A photographic analysis*. New York: New York Academy of Sciences.

Beatty, A. (2013). Current emotion research in anthropology: Reporting the field. *Emotion Review, 5*(4), 414–422.

Beatty, A. (2014). Anthropology and emotion. *Journal of the Royal Anthropological Institute, 20*(3), 545–563.

Beatty, A. (2019). *Emotional worlds: Beyond an anthropology of emotion.* Cambridge: Cambridge University Press.

Behar, R. (1996). *Vulnerable observer: Anthropology that breaks your heart.* Boston: Beacon Press.

Benedict, R. (1935). *Patterns of culture.* London: Routledge.

Bericat, E. (2016). The sociology of emotions: Four decades of progress. *Current Sociology, 64*(3), 491–513.

Berlin, B., & Kay, P. (1969). *Basic color terms: Their universality and evolution.* Berkeley: University of California Press.

Besnier, N. (1990). Language and affect. *Annual Review of Anthropology, 19,* 419–451.

Bickel, B. (2014). Linguistic diversity and universals. In N. J. Enfield, P. Kockelman, & J. Sidnell (Eds.), *The Cambridge handbook of linguistic anthropology* (pp. 102–127). Cambridge: Cambridge University Press.

Bilimoria, P., & Wenta, A. (Eds.). (2015). *Emotions in Indian thought-systems.* New York: Routledge.

Birdwhistell, R. L. (1970). *Kinesics and context: Essays on body motion communication.* Philadelphia: University of Pennsylvania Press.

Birx, J. H. (Ed.). (2010). *21st century anthropology: A reference handbook.* New York: Sage.

Bliss-Moreau, E., Williams, L. A., & Karaskiewicz, C. L. (2021). Evolution of emotion in social context. In T. K. Shackelford, & V. A. Weekes-Shackelford (Eds.), *Encyclopedia of evolutionary psychological science* (pp. 2487–2499). New York: Springer.

Boas, F. (1910). Psychological problems in anthropology. *The American Journal of Psychology, 21*(3), 371–384.

Boddice, R. (2017). The history of emotions: Past, present, future. *Revista de Estudios Sociales, 62,* 10–15.

Boddice, R. (2018). The history of emotions. In S. Handley, R. McWilliam, & L. Noakes (Eds.), *New directions in social and cultural history* (pp. 45–63). London: Bloomsbury.

Boddice, R. (2019). The developing brain as historical artifact. *Developmental Psychology, 55*(9), 1994–1997.

Boddice, R. (2020a). From the ashes, a fertile opportunity for historicism. *History of the Human Sciences, 33*(2), 126–133.

Boddice, R. (2020b). History looks forward: Interdisciplinarity and critical emotion research. *Emotion Review, 12*(3), 131–134.

Boddice, R. (2024). *The history of emotion.* 2nd ed. Manchester: Manchester University Press.

Boiger, M., & Mesquita, B. (2012a). Emotion science needs to account for the social world. *Emotion Review, 4*(3), 236–237.

Boiger, M., & Mesquita, B. (2012b). The construction of emotion in interactions, relationships, and cultures. *Emotion Review, 4*(3), 221–229.

Boiger, M., & Mesquita, B. (2015). A sociodynamic perspective on the construction of emotion. In L. F. Barrett, & J. A. Russell (Eds.), *The psychological construction of emotion* (pp. 377–398). New York: Guilford.

Boiger, M., Ceulemans, E., De Leersnyder, J., et al. (2018). Beyond essentialism: Cultural differences in emotions revisited. *Emotion, 18*(8), 1142–1162.

Bound Alberti, F. (2018). This "modern epidemic": Loneliness as an emotion cluster and a neglected subject in the history of emotion. *Emotion Review, 10* (3), 242–254.

Boyd, R., & Richerson, P. J. (1985). *Culture and the evolutionary process.* Chicago: University of Chicago.

Brady, M. S. (2024). An overview of contemporary theories of emotion in philosophy. In Scarantino, *Emotion theory*, pp. 215–231.

Briggs, J. L. (1970). *Never in anger: Portrait of an Eskimo family.* Cambridge, MA: Harvard University Press.

Brooks, J. A., Shablack, H., Gendron, M., et al. (2017). The role of language in the experience and perception of emotion: A neuroimaging meta-analysis. *Social Cognitive and Affective Neuroscience, 12*(2), 169–183.

Brooks, J. A., Chikazoe, J., Sadato, N., & Freeman, J. B. (2019). The neural representation of facial-emotion categories reflects conceptual structure. *PNAS, 116*(32), 15861–15870.

Brothers, L. (1997). *Friday's footprint: How society shapes the human mind.* Oxford: Oxford University Press.

Brown, D. (2001). Human universals. In R. A. Wilson, & F. C. Keil (Eds.), *The MIT encyclopedia of the cognitive sciences* (pp. 382–383). Cambridge, MA: The MIT Press.

Brown, D. E. (1991). *Human universals.* New York: McGraw Hill.

Brown, D. E. (2000). Human universals and their implications. In N. Roughley (Ed.), *Being humans: Anthropological universality and particularity in transdisciplinary perspective* (pp. 156–174). New York: Walter de Gruyter.

Buck, R. (2014). *Emotion: A biosocial synthesis.* Cambridge: Cambridge University Press.

Buss, D. M. (Ed.). (2015). *The handbook of evolutionary psychology.* 2 vols. Hoboken: Wiley.

Buss, D. M. (2018). Sexual and emotional infidelity: Evolved gender differences in jealousy prove robust and replicable. *Perspectives on Psychological Science, 13*(2), 155–160.

Campeggiani, P. (2023). *Theories of emotion: Expressing, feeling, acting.* London: Bloomsbury.

Camras, L. A., Fatani, S. S., Fraumeni, B. R., & Shuster, M. M. (2016). The development of facial expressions: Current perspectives on infant emotions. In Barrett, Lewis, & Haviland-Jones, *Handbook of emotions*, pp. 255–271.

Carroll, J. (2018). Evolutionary literary theory. In D. H. Richter (Ed.), *A companion to literary theory* (pp. 425–438). New York: John Wiley.

Carroll, J. (2022a). Evolution: How evolved emotions work in literary meaning. In Hogan, Irish, & Hogan, *Routledge Companion*, pp. 85–97.

Carroll, J. (2022b). Narrative theory and neuroscience: Why human nature matters. *Evolutionary Studies in Imaginative Culture, 6*(2), 81–100.

Carroll, J., Clasen, M., Jonsson, E., et al. (2018). Biocultural theory: The current state of knowledge. *Evolutionary Behavioral Sciences, 11*(1), 1–15.

Carroll, J., Clasen, M., & Jonsson, E. (Eds.). (2020). *Evolutionary perspectives on imaginative culture.* Cham: Springer.

Carroll, J. M., & Russell, J. A. (1996). Do facial expressions signal specific emotions? Judging emotion from the face in context. *Journal of Personality and Social Psychology, 70*(2), 205–218.

Carroll, N. (2022). Philosophy, literature, and emotion. In Hogan, Irish, & Hogan, *Routledge Companion*, pp. 110–120.

Celeghin, A., Diano, M., Bagnis, A., Viola, M., & Tamietto, M. (2017). Basic emotions in human neuroscience: Neuroimaging and beyond. *Frontiers in Psychology, 8*, article 1432.

Charland, L. C. (1995). Feeling and representing: Computational theory and the modularity of affect. *Synthese, 105*(3), 273–301.

Charland, L. C. (2001). In defence of "emotion." *Canadian Journal of Philosophy, 31*(1), 133–154.

Charland, L. C. (2002). The natural kind status of emotion. *The British Journal for the Philosophy of Science, 53*(4), 511–537.

Cheng, J. T., Tracy, J. L., & Henrich, J. (2010). Pride, personality, and the evolutionary foundations of human social status. *Evolution and Human Behavior, 31*(5), 334–347.

Chentsova-Dutton, Y. E., Gold, A., Gomes, A., & Ryder, A. G. (2020). Feelings in the body: Cultural variations in the somatic concomitants of affective experience. *Emotion, 20*(8), 1490–1494.

Chiao, J. Y. (Ed.). (2009). *Cultural neuroscience: Cultural influences on brain function.* Amsterdam: Elsevier.

Chiao, J. Y. (2015). Current emotion research in cultural neuroscience. *Emotion Review, 7*(3), 280–293.

Chiao, J. Y. (2018). *Philosophy of cultural neuroscience.* New York: Routledge.

Chiao, J. Y., & Immordino-Yang, M. H. (2013). Modularity and the cultural mind: Contributions of cultural neuroscience to cognitive theory. *Perspectives on Psychological Science*, *8*(1), 56–61.

Chiao, J. Y., Li, S.-C., Seligman, R., & Turner, R. (Eds.). (2016). *The Oxford handbook of cultural neuroscience*. Oxford: Oxford University Press.

Church, T., Katigbak, M. S., Reyes, J. A. S., & Jensen, S. M. (1998). Language and organisation of Filipino emotion concepts: Comparing emotion concepts and dimensions across cultures. *Cognition and Emotion*, *12*(1), 63–92.

Ciofalo, N. (Ed.). (2019). *Indigenous psychologies in an era of decolonization*. New York: Springer.

Clanton, G. (2019). Envy: Hostility towards superiors. In Jacobsen, *Emotions, everyday life and sociology*, pp. 142–156.

Clark, J. A. (2010). Relations of homology between higher cognitive emotions and basic emotions. *Biology & Philosophy*, *25*(1), 75–94.

Clark-Polner, E., Wager, T. D., Satpute, A. B., & Barrett, L. F. (2016). Neural fingerprinting: Meta-analysis, variation, and the search for brain-based essences in the science of emotion. In Barrett, Lewis, & Haviland-Jones, *Handbook of emotions*, pp. 146–165.

Clark-Polner, E., Johnson, T. D., & Barrett, L. F. (2017). Multivoxel pattern analysis does not provide evidence to support the existence of basic emotions. *Cerebral Cortex*, *27*(3), 1944–1948.

Clore, G. R. (2018). The impact of affect depends on its object. In A. S. Fox, R. C. Lapate, A. J. Shackman, and R. J. Davidson (Eds.), *The nature of emotion: Fundamental questions*, 2nd ed. (pp. 186–189). Oxford: Oxford University Press.

Cochrane, T. (2019). *The emotional mind: A control theory of affective states*. Cambridge: Cambridge University Press.

Cohen, A., & Stern, S. (Eds.). (2017). *Thinking about the emotions: A philosophical history*. Oxford: Oxford University Press.

Colombetti, G. (2009). From affect programs to dynamical discrete emotions. *Philosophical Psychology*, *22*(4), 407–425.

Colombetti, G. (2013). *The feeling body: Affective science meets the enactive mind*. Cambridge, MA: MIT Press.

Comer, C., & Taggart, A. (2021). *Brain, mind, and the narrative imagination*. London: Bloomsbury.

Cordaro, D. (2024). Basic emotion theory: A beginner's guide. In L. Al-Shawaf, & T. K. Shackelford (Eds.), *The Oxford handbook of evolution and the emotions* (pp. 3–20). Oxford: Oxford University Press.

Cordaro, D. T., Sun, R., Keltner, D. et al. (2018). Universals and cultural variations in 22 emotional expressions across five cultures. *Emotion*, *18*(1), 75–93.

Cordaro, D. T., Sun, R., Kamble, S. et al. (2020). The recognition of 18 facial-bodily expressions across nine cultures. *Emotion, 20*(7), 1292–1300.

Cosmides, L., & Tooby, J. (2000). Evolutionary psychology and the emotions. In M. Lewis, & J. M. Haviland-Jones (Eds.), *Handbook of emotions, second edition* (pp. 91–115). New York: Guilford.

Cosmides, L., & Tooby, J. (2013). Evolutionary psychology: New perspectives on cognition and motivation. *Annual Review of Psychology, 64*, 201–229.

Cowen, A. S., & Keltner, D. (2017). Self-report captures 27 distinct categories of emotion bridged by continuous gradients. *Proceedings of the National Academy of Sciences of the United States of America, 114*(38), E7900–E7909.

Cowen, A. S., & Keltner, D. (2018). Clarifying the conceptualization, dimensionality, and structure of emotion: Response to Barrett and colleagues. *Trends in Cognitive Sciences, 22*(4), 274–276.

Cowen, A. S., & Keltner, D. (2020). What the face displays: Mapping 28 emotions conveyed by naturalistic expression. *American Psychologist, 75*(3), 349–364.

Cowen, A. S., & Keltner, D. (2021). Semantic space theory: A computational approach to emotion. *Trends in Cognitive Science, 25*(2), 124–136.

Cowen, A. S., Elfenbein, H. A., Laukka, P., & Keltner, D. (2019). Mapping 24 emotions conveyed by brief human vocalization. *American Psychologist, 74*(6), 698–712.

Cowen, A. S., Sauter, D., Tracy, J. L., & Keltner, D. (2019). Mapping the passions: Toward a high-dimensional taxonomy of emotional experience and expression. *Psychological Science in the Public Interest, 20*(1), 69–90.

Cowen, A. S., Keltner, D., Schroff, F. et al. (2021). Sixteen facial expressions occur in similar contexts worldwide. *Nature, 589*(7841), 251–257.

Crawford, L. E. (2009). Conceptual metaphors of affect. *Emotion Review, 1*(2), 129–139.

Crivelli, C., Jarillo, S., Russell, J. A., & Fernández-Dols, J.-M. (2016). Reading emotions from faces in two indigenous societies. *Journal of Experimental Psychology, 145*(7), 830–843.

Cunningham, W. A., Dunfield, K. A., & Stillman, P. E. (2013). Emotional states from affective dynamics. *Emotion Review, 5*(4), 344–355.

Damasio, A. (1994). *Descartes' error: Emotion, reason, and the human brain.* New York: Putnam.

Damasio, A. (1995). Toward a neurobiology of emotion and feeling: Operational concepts and hypotheses. *The Neuroscientist, 1*(1), 19–25.

Damasio, A. (1999). *The feeling of what happens: Body and emotion in the making of consciousness.* New York: Harcourt Brace.

Damasio, A. (2003). *Looking for Spinoza: Joy, sorrow, and the feeling brain.* London: William Heinemann.

Damasio, A., & Carvalho, G. B. (2013). The nature of feelings: Evolutionary and neurobiological origins. *Nature Reviews Neuroscience, 14*(2), 143–152.

Daneš, F. (2004). Universality vs. cultural-specificity of emotion. In E. Weigand (Ed.), *Emotion in dialogic interaction* (pp. 23–32). Amsterdam: John Benjamins.

Danziger, K. (1990). Generative metaphor and the history of psychological discourse. In D. E. Leary (Ed.), *Metaphors in the history of psychology* (pp. 331–356). Cambridge: Cambridge University Press.

Darwin, C. (1872). *The expression of the emotions in man and animals.* London: John Murray .

Davies, J., & Spencer, D. (Eds.). (2010). *Emotions in the field: The psychology and anthropology of fieldwork experience.* Palo Alto: Stanford University Press.

De Leersnyder, J., Mesquita, B., & Boiger, M. (2021). What has culture got to do with emotions? (A lot). In M. J. Gelfand, C.-Y. Chiu, & Y.-Y. Hong (Eds.), *Handbook of advances in culture and psychology* (pp. 62–119). Oxford: Oxford University Press.

De Sousa, R. (1987). *The rationality of emotion.* Cambridge, MA: MIT Press.

Degli Esposti, M., Altmann, E., & Pachet, F. (2016). *Creativity and universality in language.* Cham: Springer.

Deigh, J. (Ed.). (2013). *On emotions: Philosophical essays.* Oxford: Oxford University Press.

DeLancey, C. (2002). *Passionate engines: What emotions reveal about mind and artificial intelligence.* Oxford: Oxford University Press.

Demertzis, N. (2020). *The political sociology of emotions: Essays on trauma and ressentiment.* New York: Routledge.

Deonna, J. A., & Teroni, F. (2012). *The emotions: A philosophical introduction.* New York: Routledge.

Dewaele, J.-M. (2010). *Emotions in multiple languages.* New York: Palgrave.

Dixon, T. (2020). What is the history of anger a history of? *Emotions: History, Culture, Society, 4*(1), 1–34.

Dodds, P. S., Clark, E. M., Desu, S., et al. (2015). Human language reveals a universal positivity bias. *PNAS, 112*(8), 2389–2394.

Dodman, T. (2021). Theories and methods in the history of emotions. In K. Barclay, S. Crozier-De Rosa, & P. N. Stearns (Eds.), *Sources for the history of emotions: A guide* (pp. 15–25). New York: Routledge.

Downey, G., & Gillett, A. J. (2023). Linguistic relativity in cross-cultural context: Converging evidence from neuroanthropology. *Topics in Cognitive Science*, *15*(4), 693–697.

Doyle, C. M., & Lindquist, K. A. (2018). When a word is worth a thousand pictures: Language shapes perceptual memory for emotion. *Journal of Experimental Psychology: General*, *147*(1), 62–73.

Doyle, C. M., Lane, S. T., Brooks, J. A., et al. (2022). Unsupervised classification reveals consistency and degeneracy in neural network patterns of emotion. *Social Cognitive and Affect Neuroscience*, *17*(11), 995–1006.

Durán, J. I., & Fernández-Dols, J.-M. (2021). Do emotions result in their predicted facial expressions? A meta-analysis of studies on the co-occurrence of expression and emotion. *Emotion*, *21*(7), 1550–1569.

Durán, J. I., Reisenzein, R., & Fernández-Dols, J.-M. (2017). Coherence between emotions and facial expressions: A research synthesis. In J.-M. Fernández-Dols, & J. A. Russell (Eds.), *The science of facial expression* (pp. 107–129). Oxford: Oxford University Press.

Durst, U. (2003). The natural semantic metalanguage approach to linguistic meaning. *Theoretical Linguistics*, *29*(3), 157–200.

Ekman, P. (1971). Universals and cultural differences in facial expressions of emotion. *Nebraska Symposium on Motivation*, *19*, 207–283.

Ekman, P. (1992). An argument for basic emotions. *Cognition and Emotion*, *6* (3/4), 169–200.

Ekman, P. (1993). Facial expression and emotion. *American Psychologist*, *48* (4), 384–392.

Ekman, P. (1999). Basic emotions. In T. Dalgleish, & M. J. Power (Eds.), *Handbook of cognition and emotion* (pp. 45–60). New York: Wiley.

Ekman, P. (2016). What scientists who study emotion agree about. *Perspectives on Psychological Science*, *11*(1), 31–34.

Ekman, P., & Cordaro, D. (2011). What is meant by calling emotions basic. *Emotion Review*, *3*(4), 364–370.

Ekman, P., Levenson, R. W., & Friesen, W. V. (1983). Autonomic nervous system activity distinguishes among emotions. *Science*, *221*(4616), 1208–1210.

Ekman, P., Friesen, W. V., O'Sullivan, M., et al. (1987). Universals and cultural differences in the judgments of facial expressions of emotion. *Journal of Personality and Social Psychology*, *53*(4), 712–717.

Elfenbein, H. A., & Ambady, N. (2002). On the universality and cultural specificity of emotion recognition: A meta-analysis. *Psychological Bulletin*, *128*(2), 203–235.

Ellsworth, P. C. (2024). Appraisal theories of emotions. In Scarantino, *Emotion theory*, pp. 331–349.

Emanatian, M. (1995). Metaphor and the expression of emotion: The value of cross-cultural perspectives. *Metaphor & Symbolic Activity, 10*(3), 163–182.

Epstein, A. L. (1992). *In the midst of life: Affect and ideation in the world of the Tolai.* Berkeley: University of California Press.

Eustace, N. (2008). *Passion is the gale: Emotion, power, and the coming of the American revolution.* Chapel Hill: University of North Carolina Press.

Eustace, N., Lean, E., Livingston, J., et al. (2012). AHR conversation: The historical study of emotion. *American Historical Review, 117*, 1487–1531.

Evans, N., & Levinson, S. C. (2009). The myth of language universals: Language diversity and its importance for cognitive science. *Behavioral and Brain Sciences, 32*(5), 429–448.

Fang, X., Sauter, D. A., Heerdink, M. W., & van Kleef, G. A. (2022). Culture shapes the distinctiveness of posed and spontaneous facial expressions of anger and disgust. *Journal of Cross-Cultural Psychology, 53*(5), 471–487.

Fehr, B. (1988). Prototype analysis of the concepts of love and commitment. *Journal of Personality and Social Psychology, 55*(4), 557–579.

Fehr, B. (1994). Prototype-based assessment of laypeople's views of love. *Personal Relationships, 1*(4), 309–331.

Fehr, B. (2005). The role of prototypes in interpersonal cognition. In M. W. Baldwin (Ed.), *Interpersonal cognition* (pp. 180–205). New York: Guilford.

Fehr, B., & Russell, J. A. (1984). Concept of emotion viewed from a prototype perspective. *Journal of Experimental Psychology: General, 113*(3), 464–486.

Fehr, B., & Russell, J. A. (1991). The concept of love viewed from a prototype perspective. *Journal of Personality and Social Psychology, 60*(3), 425–438.

Feldman, L. A. (1995a). Variations in the circumplex structure of mood. *Personality and Social Psychology Bulletin, 21*(8), 806–817.

Feldman, L. A. (1995b). Valence focus and arousal focus: Individual differences in the structure of affective experience. *Journal of Personality and Social Psychology, 69*(1), 153–166.

Firth-Godbehere, R. (2021). *A human history of emotion: How the way we feel built the world we know.* New York: Little, Brown, Spark.

Floman, J. L., Brackett, M. A., LaPalme, M. L., et al. (2023). Development and validation of an ability measure of emotion understanding: The core relational themes of emotion (CORE) test. *Journal of Intelligence, 11*, article 195.

Fontaine, J. J. R., Scherer, K. R., & Soriano, C. (Eds.). (2013). *Components of emotional meaning: A sourcebook.* Oxford: Oxford University Press.

Fox, A. S., Lapate, R. C., Shackman, A. J., & Davidson, R. J. (Eds.). (2018). *The nature of emotion: Fundamental questions* (2nd ed.). Oxford: Oxford University Press.

Franks, D. D. (2010). *Neurosociology.* New York: Springer.

Fridlund, A. J. (1994). *Human facial expression: An evolutionary view.* San Diego: Academic Press.

Frijda, N. H., & Parrott, W. G. (2011). Basic emotions or Ur-emotions? *Emotion Review, 3*(4), 406–415.

Gallese, V., & Wojciehowski, H. C. (2018). Embodiment and universals. *Literary Universals Project.* https://literary-universals.uconn.edu/2018/09/25/embodiment-and-universals.

Gallois, C., Vanman, E. J., Kalokerinos, E. K., & Greenaway, K. H. (2021). Emotion and its management: The lens of language and social psychology. *Journal of Language and Social Psychology, 40*(1), 42–59.

Geeraerts, D. (2006). *Words and other wonders: Papers on lexical and semantic topics.* Berlin: De Gruyter.

Geertz, C. (1962). The growth of culture and the evolution of mind. In J. M. Scher (Ed.), *Theories of the mind* (pp. 713–740). New York: Free Press.

Geertz, C. (1966). The impact of the concept of culture on the concept of man. In J. Platt, (Ed.), *New views of the nature of man* (pp. 93–118). Chicago: The University of Chicago Press.

Geertz, C. (1973). *The interpretation of cultures.* New York: Basic Books.

Geertz, C. (1975). On the nature of anthropological understanding. *American Scientist, 63*(1), 47–53.

Geertz, C. (1980). *Negara: The theatre state in nineteenth-century Bali.* Princeton: Princeton University Press.

Geertz, H. (1959). The vocabulary of emotion: A study of Javanese socialization processes. *Psychiatry, 22*(3), 225–237.

Gendron, M. (2017). Revisiting diversity: Cultural variation reveals the constructed nature of emotion perception. *Current Opinions in Psychology, 17*, 145–150.

Gendron, M., Lindquist, K. A., Barsalou, L., & Barrett, L. F. (2012). Emotion words shape emotion percepts. *Emotion, 12*(2), 314–325.

Gendron, M., Roberson, D., Van Der Vyver, J. M., & Barrett, L. F. (2014). Perceptions of emotion from facial expressions are not culturally universal: Evidence from a remote culture. *Emotion, 14*(2), 251–262.

Gendron, M., Crivelli, C., & Barrett, L. F. (2018). Universality reconsidered: Diversity in making meaning of facial expressions. *Current Directions in Psychological Science, 27*(4), 211–219.

Gerber, E. R. (1975). The cultural patterning of emotions in Samoa. Ph.D. Dissertation, University of California, San Diego.

Gerber, E. R. (1985). Rage and obligation: Samoan emotion in conflict. In G. M. White, & J. Kirkpatrick (Eds.), *Person, self, and experience:*

*Exploring pacific ethnopsychologies* (pp. 121–167). Berkeley: University of California Press.

Gladkova, A., Vanhatalo, U., & Goddard, C. (2016). The semantics of interjections: An experimental study with natural semantic metalanguage. *Applied Psycholinguistics*, *37*(4), 841–865.

Goddard, C. (2014). On "disgust." In F. H. Baider, & G. Cislaru (Eds.), *Linguistic approaches to emotions in context* (pp. 73–98). Amsterdam: John Benjamins.

Goddard, C. (2015). The complex, language-specific semantics of "surprise." *Review of Cognitive Linguistics*, *13*(2), 291–313.

Goddard, C. (2021). Natural semantic metalanguage. In W. Xu, & J. R. Taylor (Eds.), *The Routledge handbook of cognitive linguistics* (pp. 93–110). New York: Routledge.

Goetz, J. L., Keltner, D., & Simon-Thomas, E. (2010). Compassion: An evolutionary analysis and empirical review. *Psychological Bulletin*, *136*(3), 351–374.

Goldie, P. (2002). *The emotions: A philosophical exploration*. Oxford: Oxford University Press.

Goldie, P. (Ed.). (2010). *Oxford handbook of philosophy of emotion*. Oxford: Oxford University Press.

Gordon, S. L. (1981). The sociology of sentiments and emotion. In M. Rosenberg, & R. H. Turner (Eds.), *Social psychology: Sociological perspectives* (pp. 551–575). New York: Basic Books.

Gordon, S. L. (1990). Social structural effects on emotions. In T. D. Kemper (Ed.), *Research agendas in the sociology of emotions* (pp. 145–179). Albany: SUNY Press.

Grady, J. (1997). Foundations of meaning: Primary metaphors and primary scenes. PhD Thesis, University of California, Berkeley.

Grady, J. (2007). Metaphor. In D. Geeraerts, & H. Cuyckens (Eds.), *The Oxford handbook of cognitive linguistics* (pp. 188–213). Oxford: Oxford University Press.

Greenberg, J. H. (1975). Research on language universals. *Annual Review of Anthropology*, *4*, 75–94.

Gregg, M., & Seigworth, G. J. (Eds.). (2010). *The affect theory reader*. Durham: Duke University Press.

Griffiths, P. E. (1997). *What emotions really are*. Chicago: University of Chicago Press.

Griffiths, P. E. (2001). Emotion and the problem of psychological categories. In A. W. Kaszniak (Ed.), *Emotions, qualia, and consciousness* (pp. 28–41). Singapore: World Scientific.

Griffiths, P. E. (2004a). Emotions as natural and normative kinds. *Philosophy of Science*, *71*(5), 901–911.

Griffiths, P. E. (2004b). Is emotion a natural kind? In R. C. Solomon (Ed.), *Thinking about feeling: Contemporary philosophers on emotions* (pp. 233–249). Oxford: Oxford University Press.

Griffiths, P. E. (2017). Current emotion research in philosophy. In R. Kingston, K. Banerjee, J. McKee, Y. -C. Chien, and C. C. Vassiliou (Eds.), *Emotions, community, and citizenship* (pp. 107–125). Toronto: University of Toronto Press.

Grima, B. (1992). *The performance of emotion among Paxtun women*. Austin: University of Texas Press.

Gross, D. M. (2010). Defending the humanities with Charles Darwin's *The expression of the emotions in man and animals* (1872). *Critical Inquiry, 37* (1), 34–59.

Guillory, S. A., & Bujarski, K. A. (2014). Exploring emotions using invasive methods: Review of 60 years of human intracranial electrophysiology. *Social Cognitive and Affective Neuroscience, 9*(12), 1180–1889.

Han, S. (2017). *The sociocultural brain: A cultural neuroscience approach to human nature*. Oxford: Oxford University Press.

Han, S., Northoff, G., Vogeley, K., et al. (2013). A cultural neuroscience approach to the biosocial nature of the human brain. *Annual Review of Psychology, 64*(1), 335–359.

Harkins, J., & Wierzbicka, A. (Eds.). (2001). *Emotions in crosslinguistic perspective*. Berlin: De Gruyter.

Harré, R. (1986). An outline of the social constructivist viewpoint. In R. Harré (Ed.), *The social construction of emotions* (pp. 2–14). Oxford: Basil Blackwell.

Harré, R. (2000). Encountering the other through grammar. In N. Roughley (Ed.), *Being humans: Anthropological universality and particularity in transdisciplinary perspectives* (pp. 107–130). Berlin: De Gruyter.

Harré, R., & Llored, J. P. (2018). Contingent universals as the expression of a culture. In G. Jovanović, L. Allolio-Näcke, & C. Ratner (Eds.), *The challenges of cultural psychology: Historical legacies and future responsibilities* (pp. 189–206). New York: Routledge.

Harris, S. R. (2015). *An invitation to the sociology of emotions*. New York: Routledge.

Heider, K. G. (2011). *The cultural context of emotion: Folk psychology in West Sumatra*. New York: Palgrave.

Henrich, J., Heine, S. J., & Norenzayan, A. (2010). The weirdest people in the world? *Behavioral and Brain Sciences, 33*(2–3), 61–83.

Hermann, D. J., & Raybeck, D. (1981). Similarities and differences in meaning in six cultures. *Journal of Cross-Cultural Psychology, 12*(2), 194–206.

Hess, U., & Hareli, S. (Eds.). (2019). *The social nature of emotion expression: What emotions can tell us about the world*. New York: Springer.

Hochschild, A. (1983a). Comment on Kemper's "Social constructionist and positivist approaches to the sociology of emotion." *American Journal of Sociology, 89*(2), 432–434.

Hochschild, A. R. (1979). Emotion work, feeling rules, and social structure. *American Journal of Sociology, 85*(3), 551–575.

Hochschild, A. R. (1983b). *The managed heart: Commercialization of human feeling*. Berkeley: University of California Press.

Hochschild Denzin, N. K. (1990). On understanding emotion: The interpretive-cultural agenda. In T. D. Kemper (Ed.), *Research agendas in the sociology of emotion* (pp. 85–116). Albany: SUNY Press.

Hoemann, K., Khan, Z., Feldman, M. J., et al. (2020). Context-aware experience sampling reveals the scale of variation in affective experience. *Science Report, 10*(1), article 12459.

Hoemann, K., Gendron, M., Crittenden, A. N., et al. (2024). What we can learn about emotion by talking with the Hadza. *Perspectives on Psychological Science, 19*(1), 173–200.

Hogan, L. P. (2011). Dhvani and rasa. In P. Hogan (Ed.), *The Cambridge encyclopedia of the language sciences* (pp. 251–252). Cambridge: Cambridge University Press.

Hogan, P. C. (2003). *The mind and its stories: Narrative universals and human emotion*. Cambridge: Cambridge University Press.

Hogan, P. C. (2008a). For evolutionary criticism, against genetic absolutism. *Style, 42*(2–3), 202–206.

Hogan, P. C. (2008b). Of literary universals: Ninety-five theses. *Philosophy and Literature, 32*(1), 145–160.

Hogan, P. C. (2011a). *Affective narratology: The emotional structure of stories*. Lincoln: University of Nebraska Press.

Hogan, P. C. (2011b). *What literature teaches us about emotion*. Cambridge: Cambridge University Press.

Hogan, P. C. (2013). *How authors' minds make stories*. Cambridge: Cambridge University Press.

Hogan, P. C. (2018). *Literature and emotion*. New York: Routledge.

Hogan, P. C. (2022). Stories: Particular causes and universal genres. In Hogan, Irish, & Hogan, *Routledge companion*, pp. 328–339.

Hogan, P. C., Irish, B. J., & Hogan, L. P. (Eds.). (2022). *The Routledge companion to literature and emotion*. New York: Routledge.

Horikawa, T., Cowen, A. S., Keltner, D., & Kamitani, Y. (2020). The neural representation of visually evoked emotion is high-dimensional, categorical, and distributed across transmodal brain regions. *iScience, 23*(5), article 101060.

Huang, Y.-A., Jastorff, J., Van den Stock, J., et al. (2018). Studying emotion theories through connectivity analysis: Evidence from generalized psychophysiological interactions and graph theory. *NeuroImage, 172*, 260–262.

Huntington, R., & Metcalf, P. (1979). *Celebrations of death: The anthropology of mortuary ritual*. Cambridge: Cambridge University Press.

Hupka, R. B., Lenton, A. P., & Hutchison, K. A. (1999). Universal development of emotion categories in natural language. *Journal of Personality and Social Psychology, 77*(2), 247–278.

Hwang, H. C., & Matsumoto, D. (2015). Evidence for the universality of facial expressions of emotion. In M. K. Mandal, & A. Awasthi (Eds.), *Understanding facial expressions in communication: Cross-cultural and multidisciplinary perspectives* (pp. 41–56). New York: Springer.

Hwang, H. C., & Matsumoto, D. (2020). Cross-cultural emotional expression. In B. J. Carducci, & C. S. Nave (Eds.), *The Wiley encyclopedia of personality and individual differences*. 4 vols. (pp. 4.257–263). Hoboken: John Wiley & Sons.

Illouz, E., & Wilf, E. (2009). Hearts of wombs? A cultural critique of radical feminist critiques of love. In D. Hopkins, J. Kleres, H. Flam, and H. Kuzmics (Eds.), *Theorizing emotions: sociological explorations and applications* (pp. 121–142). New York: Campus Verlag.

Immordino-Yang, M. H., & Yang, X.-F. (2017). Cultural differences in the neural correlates of social-emotional feelings: An interdisciplinary, developmental perspective. *Current Opinion in Psychology, 17*, 34–40.

Immordino-Yang, M. H., Yang, X. F., & Damasio, H. (2014). Correlations between social-emotional feelings and anterior insula activity are independent from visceral states but influenced by culture. *Frontiers in Human Neuroscience, 8*, article 728.

Irish, B. J. (2018). *Emotion in the Tudor court: Literature, history, and early modern feeling*. Evanston: Northwestern University Press.

Irish, B. J. (2020). A strategic compromise: Universality, interdisciplinarity, and the case for modal emotions in history of emotion research. *Emotions: History, Culture, Society, 4*(2), 231–251.

Irish, B. J. (2023). *Shakespeare and disgust: The history and science of early modern revulsion*. London: Bloomsbury.

Israelashvili, J., Hassin, R. R., & Aviezer, H. (2019). When emotions run high: A critical role for context in the unfolding of dynamic, real-life facial affect. *Emotion, 19*(3), 558–562.

Izard, C. E. (1971). *The face of emotion*. New York: Appleton-Century-Crofts.

Izard, C. E. (1977). *Human emotions*. New York: Plenum Press.

Izard, C. E. (1991). *The psychology of emotions*. New York: Plenum Press.

Izard, C. E. (1994). Innate and universal facial expressions: Evidence from developmental and cross-cultural research. *Psychological Bulletin, 115*(2), 288–299.

Izard, C. E. (2007). Basic emotions, natural kinds, emotion schemas, and a new paradigm. *Perspectives on Psychological Science, 2*(3), 260–280.

Izard, C. E. (2009). Emotion theory and research: Highlights, unanswered questions, and emerging issues. *Annual Review of Psychology, 60*, 1–25.

Izard, C. E. (2011). Forms and functions of emotions: Matters of emotion-cognition interactions. *Emotion Review, 3*(4), 371–378.

Jack, R. E., Garrod, O. G. B., Yu, H., Caldara, R., & Schyns, P. G. (2012). Facial expressions of emotion are not culturally universal. *PNAS, 109*(19), 7241–7244.

Jacobsen, M. H. (Ed.). (2019). *Emotions, everyday life and sociology.* New York: Routledge.

Jacobsen, M. H., & Kristiansen, S. (2019). Embarrassment: Experience awkward self-awareness in everyday life. In Jacobsen, *Emotions, everyday life and sociology*, pp. 104–125.

James, W. (1884). What is an emotion? *Mind, 9*(34), 188–205.

James, W. (1890). *The principles of psychology.* 2 vols. New York: Holt.

Johnson-Laird, P. N., & Oatley, K. (2022). How poetry evokes emotions. *Acta Psychologica, 224*, article 103506.

Johnston, E., & Olson, L. (2015). *The feeling brain: The biology and psychology of emotions.* New York: Norton.

Jonsson, E. (2020). Evolutionary literary theory. In T. K. Shackelford (Ed.), *The SAGE handbook of evolutionary psychology* (pp. 403–420). Thousand Oaks: SAGE.

Jonsson, E. (2021). *The early evolutionary imagination: Literature and human nature.* New York: Palgrave.

Juslin, P. N., & Laukka, P. (2003). Communication of emotions in vocal expression and music performance: Different channels, same code? *Psychological Bulletin, 129*(5), 770–814.

Kamiloğlu, R. G., Cong, Y., Sun, R., & Sauter, D. A. (2024). Emotions across cultures. In L. Al-Shawaf, & T. K. Shackelford (Eds.), *The Oxford handbook of evolution and the emotions* (pp. 983–996). Oxford: Oxford University Press.

Keith, K. D. (2019). Psychology and culture: An introduction. In K. D. Keith (Ed.), *Cross-cultural psychology: Contemporary themes and perspectives* (pp. 3–22). New York: Wiley Blackwell.

Keltner, D., & Cordaro, D. T. (2017). Understanding multimodal emotional expressions: Recent advances in basic emotion theory. In J.-M. Fernández-Dols, & J. A. Russell (Eds.), *The science of facial expression* (pp. 57–75). Oxford: Oxford University Press.

Keltner, D., Haidt, J., & Shiota, M. N. (2006). Social functionalism and the evolution of emotions. In M. Schaller, J. A. Simpson, & D. T. Kenrick (Eds.), *Evolution and social psychology* (pp. 115–142). New York: Psychology Press.

Keltner, D., Sauter, D., Tracy, J., & Cowen, A. (2019). Emotional expression: Advances in basic emotion theory. *Journal of Nonverbal Behavior, 43*(2), 133–160.

Keltner, D., Tracy, J. L., Sauter, D., & Cowen, A. (2019). What basic emotion theory really says for the twenty-first century study of emotion. *Journal of Nonverbal Behavior, 43*(2), 195–201.

Keltner, D., Sauter, D., Tracy, J. L., Wetchler, E., & Cowen, A. S. (2022). How emotions, relationships, and culture constitute each other: Advances in social functionalist theory. *Cognition and Emotion, 36*(3), 388–401.

Keltner, D., Brooks, J. A., & Cowen, A. (2023). Semantic space theory: Data-driven insights into basic emotions. *Current Directions in Psychological Science, 32*(3), 242–249.

Kemper, T. D. (1978). *A social interactional theory of emotions.* New York: Wiley.

Kemper, T. D. (1981). Social constructionist and positivist approaches to the sociology of emotions. *American Journal of Sociology, 87*(2), 336–362.

Kemper, T. D. (1987). How many emotions are there? Wedding the social and autonomic components. *American Journal of Sociology, 93*(2), 263–289.

Kemper, T. D. (1990). Themes and variations in the sociology of emotions. In T. D. Kemper, (Ed.), *Research agendas in the sociology of emotion* (pp. 3–23). Albany: SUNY Press.

Kemper, T. D. (2006). Power and status and the power-status theory of emotions. In Stets & Turner, *Handbook of the sociology of emotions*, pp. 87–113.

Kemper, T. D., & Collins, R. (1990). Dimensions of microinteraction. *American Journal of Sociology, 96*(1), 32–68.

Kidron, Y., & Kuzar, R. (2002). My face is paling against my will: Emotion and control in English and Hebrew. *Pragmatics & Cognition, 10*(1–2), 129–157.

Kim, Ŭ., Yang, G., & Hwang, K. (2006). *Indigenous and cultural psychology: Understanding people in context.* New York: Springer.

Kirchner, A., Boiger, M., Uchida, Y., et al. (2018). Humiliated fury is not universal: The co-occurrence of anger and shame in the United States and Japan. *Cognition and Emotion, 32*(6), 1317–1328.

Kleres, J. (2009). Preface: Notes on the sociology of emotions in Europe. In D. Hopkins, J. Kleres, H. Flam, and H. Kuzmics (Eds.), *Theorizing emotions: Sociological explorations and applications* (pp. 7–27). New York: Campus Verlag.

Knatz, J. (2023). History of emotions and intellectual history. In S. Geroulanos, & G. Sapiro (Eds.), *The Routledge handbook of the history and sociology of ideas*. New York: Routledge, pp. 275–291.

Kollareth, D., Fernández-Dols, J.-M., & Russell, J. A. (2018). Shame as a culture-specific emotion concept. *Journal of Cognition and Culture, 18*(3–4), 274–292.

Kövecses, Z. (2000a). The concept of anger: Universal or culture specific? *Psychopathology, 33*(4), 159–170.

Kövecses, Z. (2000b). *Metaphor and emotion: Language, culture, and body in human feeling*. Cambridge: Cambridge University Press.

Kragel, P. A., & LaBar, K. S. (2013). Multivariate pattern classification reveals autonomic and experiential representations of discrete emotions. *Emotion, 13*(4), 681–690.

Kragel, P. A., & LaBar, K. S. (2014). Advancing emotion theory with multivariate pattern classification. *Emotion Review, 6*(2), 160–174.

Kragel, P. A., & LaBar, K. S. (2015). Multivariate neural biomarkers of emotional states are categorically distinct. *Social Cognitive and Affective Neuroscience, 10*(11), 1437–1448.

Kragel, P. A., & LaBar, K. S. (2016). Decoding the nature of emotion in the brain. *Trends in Cognitive Sciences, 20*(6), 444–455.

Kreibig, S. D. (2010). Autonomic nervous system activity in emotion: A review. *Biological Psychology, 84*(3), 394–421.

Kret, M. E., Prochazkova, E., Sterck, E. H. M., & Clay, Z. (2020). Emotional expressions in human and non-human great apes. *Neuroscience and Biobehavioral Reviews, 115*, 378–395.

Labarre, W. (1947). The cultural basis of emotions and gestures. *Journal of Personality, 16*(1), 49–68.

Lakoff, G. (1987). *Women, fire, and dangerous things: What categories reveal about the mind*. Chicago: University of Chicago Press.

Lakoff, G. (2014). Mapping the brain's metaphor circuitry: Metaphorical thought in everyday reason. *Frontiers in Human Neuroscience, 8*, article 958.

Lakoff, G., & Johnson, M. (1980). *Metaphors we live by*. Chicago: University of Chicago Press.

Lakoff, G., & Kövecses, Z. (1987). The cognitive model of anger inherent in American English. In D. Holland, & N. Quinn (Eds.), *Cultural models in language and thought* (pp. 195–221). Cambridge: Cambridge University Press.

Lane, R. D., Reiman, E. M., Ahern, G. L., Schwartz, G. E., & Davidson, R. J. (1997). Neuroanatomical correlates of happiness, sadness, and disgust. *American Journal of Psychiatry, 154*(7), 926–933.

Lang, P. J. (2014). Emotion's response patterns: The brain and the autonomic nervous system. *Emotion Review, 6*(2), 93–99.

Lange, J., & Zickfeld, J. H. (2021). Emotions as overlapping causal networks of emotion components: Implications and methodological approaches. *Emotion Review, 13*(2), 157–167.

Lange, J., Dalege, J., Borsboom, D., van Kleef, G. A., & Fischer, A. H. (2020). Toward an integrative psychometric model of emotions. *Perspectives on Psychological Science, 15*(2), 444–468.

Laukka, P., & Elfenbein, H. A. (2021). Cross-cultural emotion recognition and in-group advantages in vocal expression: A meta-analysis. *Emotion Review, 13*(1), 3–11.

Lazarus, R. S. (1991). *Emotion and adaptation*. Oxford: Oxford University Press.

Leach, E. (1981). A poetics of power. *The New Republic, 184*(14), 30–33.

Leavitt, J. (1996). Meaning and feeling in the anthropology of emotions. *American Ethnologist, 23*(3), 154–539.

Lebra, T. S. (1976). *Japanese patterns of behavior*. Honolulu: University of Hawaii Press.

LeDoux, J. E. (1996). *The emotional brain: The mysterious underpinnings of emotional life*. New York: Simon & Schuster.

LeDoux, J. E. (2000). Emotion circuits in the brain. *Annual Review of Neuroscience, 23*, 155–184.

LeDoux, J. E. (2012). Evolution of human emotion: A view through fear. *Progress in Brain Research, 195*, 431–442.

Lee, D. H., & Anderson, A. K. (2016). Form and function in facial expressive behavior. In Barrett, Lewis, & Haviland-Jones, *Handbook of emotions*, pp. 495–509.

Levenson, R. W. (1999). The intrapersonal functions of emotion. *Cognition and Emotion, 13*(5), 481–504.

Levenson, R. W. (2003). Autonomic specificity and emotion. In R. J. Davidson, K. R. Scherer, & H. H. Goldsmith (Eds.), *Handbook of affective sciences* (pp. 212–224). Oxford: Oxford University Press.

Levenson, R. W. (2011). Basic emotion questions. *Emotion Review, 3*(4), 379–386.

Levenson, R. W. (2014). The autonomic nervous system and emotion. *Emotion Review, 6*(2), 100–112.

Levenson, R. W., Ekman, P., & Friesen, W. V. (1990). Voluntary facial action generates emotion-specific autonomic nervous system activity. *Psychophysiology, 27*(4), 363–384.

Levenson, R. W., Ekman, P., Heider, K., & Friesen, W. V. (1992). Emotion and autonomic nervous system activity in the Minangkabau of West Sumatra. *Journal of Personality and Social Psychology, 62*(6), 972–988.

Levy, R. I. (1973). *Tahitians: Mind and experience in the society islands.* Chicago: University of Chicago Press.

Levy, R. I. (1984). Emotion, knowing, and culture. In Shweder, & LeVine, *Culture Theory,* pp. 214–237.

Lewis, D. M. G., Al-Shawaf, L., Conroy-Beam, D., Asao, K., & Buss, D. M. (2017). Evolutionary psychology: A how-to guide. *American Psychologist, 72*(4), 353–373.

Lewis, M. D., & Liu, Z. (2011). Three time scales of neural self-organization underlying basic and nonbasic emotions. *Emotion Review, 3*(4), 416–423.

Leys, R. (2017). *The ascent of affect: Genealogy and critique.* Chicago: University of Chicago Press.

Leys, R. (2021). The trouble with affect. *History of Psychology, 24*(2), 127–129.

Lindholm, C. (2007). An anthropology of emotion. In C. Conerly, & R. B. Edgerton (Eds.), *A Companion to psychological anthropology: Modernity and psychocultural change* (pp. 30–47). Oxford: Blackwell.

Lindquist, K. A. (2013). Emotions emerge from more basic psychological ingredients: A modern psychological constructionist model. *Emotion Review, 5*(4), 356–368.

Lindquist, K. A., & Barrett, L. F. (2008). Constructing emotion: The experience of fear as a conceptual act. *Psychological Science, 19*(9), 898–903.

Lindquist, K. A., & Barrett, L. F. (2012). A functional architecture of the human brain: Emerging insights from the science of emotion. *Trends in Cognitive Sciences, 16*(11), 533–540.

Lindquist, K. A., Barrett, L. F., Bliss-Moreau, E., & Russell, J. A. (2006). Language and the perception of emotion. *Emotion, 6*(1), 125–138.

Lindquist, K. A., Wager, T. D., Kober, H., Bliss-Moreau, E., & Barrett, L. F. (2012). The brain basis of emotion: A meta-analytic review. *Behaviorial and Brain Science, 35,* 121–143.

Lindquist, K. A., Siegel, E. H., Quigley, K. S., & Barrett, L. F. (2013). The hundred-year emotion war: Are emotions natural kinds or psychological constructions? Comment on lench, flores, and bench (2011). *Psychological Bulletin, 139*(1), 255–263.

Lindquist, K. A., Jackson, J. C., Leshin, J., Satpute, A. B., & Gendron, M. (2022). The cultural evolution of emotion. *Nature Reviews Psychology, 1* (11), 669–681.

Lively, K. J. (2024). An overview of contemporary theories of emotions in sociology. In Scarantino, *Emotion theory,* pp. 287–309.

Lo Bosco, M. C. (2021). Feelings in the field: The emotional labour of the ethnographer. *Anthropology in Action, 28*(2), 8–17.

Loderer, K., Gentsch, K., Duffy, M. C., et al. (2020). Are concepts of achievement-related emotions universal across cultures? A semantic profiling approach. *Cognition and Emotion, 34*(7), 1480–1488.

Long, W. J. (1909). *English literature: Its history and its significance for the life of the English-speaking world.* Boston: Ginn.

Longo, M. (2020). *Emotions through literature: Fictional narratives, society, and the emotional self.* New York: Routledge.

Lonner, W. J. (1980). The search for psychological universals. In H. C. Triandis, & W. W. Lambert (Eds.), *Handbook of cross-cultural psychology, Vol. 1* (pp. 143–204). Boston: Allyn & Bacon.

Lutz, C. (1982). The domain of emotion words on Ifaluk. *American Ethnologist, 9*(1), 113–128.

Lutz, C. (1986). Emotion, thought, and estrangement: Emotion as a cultural category. *Cultural Anthropology, 1*(3), 287–309.

Lutz, C. (1988). *Unnatural emotions: Everyday sentiments on a Micronesian atoll & their challenge to western theory.* Chicago: University of Chicago Press.

Lutz, C. (2017). What matters. *Cultural Anthropology, 32*(2), 181–191.

Lutz, C., & White, G. M. (1986). The anthropology of emotions. *Annual Review of Anthropology, 15*, 405–436.

Lynch, O. M. (1990). The social construction of emotion in India. In O. M. Lynch (Ed.), *Divine passions: The social construction of emotion in India* (pp. 3–34). Berkeley: University of California Press.

Lyon, M. L. (1995). Missing emotion: The limitations of cultural constructionism in the study of emotion. *Cultural Anthropology, 10*(2), 244–263.

MacKinnon, N. J. (1994). *Symbolic interactionism as affect control.* Albany: State University of New York Press.

Majeed, R. (2023). Does the problem of variability justify Barrett's emotion revolution? *Review of Philosophy and Psychology, 14*(4), 1421–1441.

Majid, A. (2012). Current emotion research in the language sciences. *Emotion Review, 4*(4), 432–443.

Manokara, K., & Sauter, D. A. (forthcoming). Emotion universals: The foundation from which cultural variability of emotion emerges. In J. De Leersnyder (Ed.), *The socio-cultural shaping of emotion.* Cambridge: Cambridge University Press.

Manokara, K., Đurić, M., Fischer, A., & Sauter, D. (2021). Do people agree on how positive emotions are expressed? A survey of four emotions and five modalities across 11 cultures. *Journal of Nonverbal Behavior, 45*(4), 601–632.

Markus, H. R., & Kitayama, S. (1991). Culture and the self: Implications for cognition, emotion, and motivation. *Psychological Review, 98*(2), 224–253.

Marvasti, A. B. (2019). Courage: It's not all about overcoming fear. In Jacobsen, *Emotions, everyday life and sociology*, pp. 71–87.

Mason, W. A., & Capitanio, J. P. (2012). Basic emotions: A reconstruction. *Emotion Review, 4*(3), 238–244.

Matsumoto, D. (1990). Cultural similarities and differences in display rules. *Motivation and Emotion, 14*(3), 195–214.

Matsumoto, D. (1992). American-Japanese cultural differences in the recognition of universal facial expressions. *Journal of Cross-Cultural Psychology, 23*(1), 72–84.

Matsumoto, D., & Ekman, P. (1989). American-Japanese cultural differences in intensity ratings of facial expressions of emotion. *Motivation and Emotion, 13*(2), 143–157.

Matsumoto, D., & Hwang, H. C. (2019). Culture and emotion: Integrating biological universality with cultural specificity. In D. Matsumoto, & H. C. Hwang (Eds.), *The handbook of culture and psychology* (pp. 361–398). Oxford: Oxford University Press.

Matsumoto, D., & Hwang, H. S. (2012). Culture and emotion: The integration of biological and cultural contributions. *Journal of Cross-Cultural Psychology, 43*(1), 91–118.

Matsumoto, D., & Willingham, B. (2006). The thrill of victory and the agony of defeat: Spontaneous expression of medal winners of the 2004 Athens Olympic Games. *Journal of Personality and Social Psychology, 91*(3), 568–581.

Matsumoto, D., & Wilson, M. (2022). A half-century assessment of the study of culture and emotion. *Journal of Cross-Cultural Psychology, 53*(7–8), 917–934.

Matsunaka, Y., Chen, Y., & Shinohara, K. (2023). Fluidity in Japanese emotion metaphors: A corpus study. The 16th International Cognitive Linguistics Conference, Düsseldorf, Germany. August 7–11, https://iclc16.github.io/abstracts/ICLC16_paper_185.pdf.

Matt, S. J., & Stearns, P. N. (Eds.). (2013). *Doing emotions history*. Urbana: University of Illinois Press.

Matthewson, L. (2003). Is the meta-language really natural? *Theoretical Linguistics, 29*(3), 263–274.

Mauss, I. B., & Robinson, M. D. (2009). Measures of emotion: A review. *Cognition and Emotion, 23*(2), 209–237.

Mead, M. (1928). *Coming of age in Samoa: A psychological study of primitive youth for western civilisation*. New York: William Morrow.

Mead, M. (1930). *Growing up in New Guinea*. New York: Blue Ribbon Books.

Mead, M. (1935). *Sex and temperament in three primitive societies*. New York: William Morrow.

Mendes, W. B. (2016). Emotion and the autonomic nervous system. In Barrett, Lewis, & Haviland-Jones, *Handbook of Emotions*, pp. 166–181.

Mendes, W. B., & Park, J. (2014). Neurobiological concomitants of motivational states. *Advances in Motivational Science, 1*, 233–270.

Menninghaus, W., Wagner, V., Wassiliwizky, E., et al. (2019). What are aesthetic emotions? *Psychological Review, 26*(2), 171–195.

Mesoudi, A. (2016). Cultural evolution: A review of theory, findings, and controversies. *Evolutionary Biology, 43*(4), 481–497.

Mesquita, B. (2001). Culture and emotion: Different approaches to the question. In T. J. Mayne, & G. A. Bonanno (Eds.), *Emotions: Current issues and future directions* (pp. 214–250). New York: Guilford.

Mesquita, B. (2022). *Between us: How cultures create emotions*. New York: Norton.

Mesquita, B., & Boiger, M. (2014). Emotions in context: A sociodynamic model of emotions. *Emotion Review, 6*(4), 298–302.

Mesquita, B., & Frijda, N. H. (1992). Cultural variations in emotions: A review. *Psychological Bulletin, 112*(2), 179–204.

Mesquita, B., & Parkinson, B. (2024). Social constructionist theories of emotion. In Scarantino, *Emotion theory*, pp. 388–407.

Mesquita, B., Boiger, M., & De Leersnyder, J. (2016). The cultural construction of emotions. *Current Opinion in Psychology, 8*, 31–36.

Mesquita, B., Boiger, M., & De Leersnyder, J. (2017). Doing emotions: The role of culture in everyday emotions. *European Review of Social Psychology, 28* (1), 95–133.

Milton, K. (2005). Emotion (or life, the universe, everything). *The Australian Journal of Anthropology, 16*(2), 198–211.

Montag, C., & Davis, K. L. (2020). *Animal emotions: How they drive human behavior*. Santa Barbara: Brainstorm Books.

Montag, C., & Panksepp, J. (2016). Primal emotional-affective expressive foundations of human facial expression. *Motivation and Emotion, 40*(5), 760–766.

Moore, C. C., Romney, A. K., Hsia, T.-L., & Rusch, C. D. (1999). The universality of the semantic structure of emotion terms: Methods for the study of inter- and intra-cultural variability. *American Anthropologist, 101*(3), 529–546.

Moors, A. (2014). Flavors of appraisal theories of emotion. *Emotion Review, 6* (4), 303–307.

Moors, A. (2022). *Demystifying emotions: A typology of theories in psychology and philosophy*. Cambridge: Cambridge University Press.

Mousley, A. (2007). *Re-humanising Shakespeare: Literary humanism, wisdom and modernity.* Edinburgh: Edinburgh University Press.

Mousley, A. (Ed.). (2011). *Towards a new literary humanism.* New York: Palgrave.

Murphy, F. C., Nimmo-Smith, I., & Lawrence, A. D. (2003). Functional neuro-anatomy of emotions: A meta-analysis. *Cognitive, Affective, & Behavioral Neuroscience, 3*(3), 207–233.

Myers, F. R. (1979). Emotions and the self: A theory of personhood and political order among Pintupi Aborigines. *Ethos, 7*(4), 343–370.

Nelson, N., & Russell, J. A. (2013). Universality revisited. *Emotion Review, 5* (1), 8–15.

Nesse, R. M. (1990). Evolutionary explanations of emotions. *Human Nature, 1* (3), 261–289.

Nesse, R. M., & Ellsworth, P. C. (2009). Evolution, emotions, and emotional disorders. *American Psychology, 64*(2), 129–139.

Norenzayan, A., & Heine, S. J. (2005). Psychological universals: What are they and how can we know? *Psychological Bulletin, 131*(5), 763–784.

Nummenmaa, L., & Saarimäki, H. (2019). Emotions as discrete patterns of systemic activity. *Neuroscience Letters, 693*, 3–8.

Nussbaum, M. (2001). *Upheavals of thought: The intelligence of emotion.* Cambridge: Cambridge University Press.

Oatley, K. (1993). Social construction in emotions. In M. Lewis, & J. M. Haviland (Eds.), *Handbook of emotions* (pp. 341–352). New York: Guilford.

Oatley, K. (2006). Simulation of substance and shadow: Inner emotions and outer behavior in Shakespeare's psychology of character. *College Literature, 33*(1), 15–33.

Oatley, K. (2011). *Such stuff as dreams: The psychology of fiction.* Malden: Wiley-Blackwell.

Oatley, K. (2012). *The passionate muse: Exploring emotion in stories.* Oxford: Oxford University Press.

Oatley, K. (2016). Fiction: Simulation of social worlds. *Trends in Cognitive Science, 20*(8), 618–628.

Oatley, K., & Johnson-Laird, P. N. (2011). Basic emotions in social relationships, reasoning, and psychological illnesses. *Emotion Review, 3*(4), 424–433.

Ogren, M., & Sandhofer, C. M. (2022). Emotion words link faces to emotional scenarios in early childhood. *Emotion, 22*(1), 167–178.

Ortony, A. (2022). Are all "basic emotions" emotions? A problem for the (basic) emotions construct. *Perspectives on Psychological Science, 17*(1), 41–61.

Ortony, A., & Fainsilber, L. (1989). The role of metaphors in descriptions of emotions. In Y. Wilks (Ed.), *Theoretical issues in natural language processing* (pp. 78–182). Hillsdale: Erlbaum.

Ortony, A., & Turner, T. J. (1990). What's basic about basic emotions? *Psychological Review, 97*(3), 315–331.

Ortony, A., Clore, G. L., & Collins, A. (1988). *The cognitive structure of emotions.* Cambridge: Cambridge University Press.

Özkarar-Gradwohl, F. G. (2019). Cross-cultural affective neuroscience. *Frontiers in Psychology, 10,* article 794.

Panksepp, J. (1998). *Affective neuroscience: The foundations of human and animal emotions.* Oxford: Oxford University Press.

Panksepp, J. (2005). Affective consciousness: Core emotional feelings in animals and humans. *Consciousness and Cognition, 14*(1), 30–80.

Panksepp, J. (2011). The basic emotional circuits of mammalian brains: Do animals have affective lives? *Neuroscience and Biobehavioral Reviews, 35* (9), 1791–1804.

Panksepp, J. (2012). My reflections on commentaries and concluding perspectives. In P. Zachar, & R. D. Ellis (Eds.), *Categorical versus dimensional models of affect: A seminar on the theories of Panksepp and Russell* (pp. 301–320). Amsterdam: John Benjamins.

Panksepp, J., & Biven, L. (2012). *The archaeology of mind: Neuroevolutionary origins of human emotion.* New York: Norton.

Panksepp, J., & Watt, D. (2011). What is basic about basic emotions? Lasting lessons from affective neuroscience. *Emotion Review, 3*(4), 387–396.

Paredes-Canilao, N., Babaran-Diaz, Ma. A., Florendo, Ma. N. B., & Salinas-Ramos, T. (2015). Indigenous psychologies and critical-emancipatory psychology. In I. Parker (Ed.), *Handbook of critical psychology* (pp. 356–365). New York: Routledge.

Parkinson, B. (2012). Piecing together emotion: Sites and time-scales for social construction. *Emotion Review, 4*(3), 291–298.

Parr, L. A., Waller, B. M., Vick, S. J., & Bard, K. A. (2007). Classifying chimpanzee facial expressions using muscle action. *Emotion, 7*(1), 172–181.

Parrott, W. G. (2010). Ur-emotions and your emotions: Reconceptualizing *basic emotion. Emotion Review, 2*(1), 14–21.

Parrott, W. G. (2012). Ur-emotions: The common feature of animal emotions and socially constructed emotions. *Emotion Review, 4*(3), 247–248.

Pavlenko, A. (2005). *Emotions and multilingualism.* Cambridge: Cambridge University Press.

Pavlenko, A. (Ed.). (2006). *Bilingual minds: Emotional experience, expression, and representation.* Buffalo: Multilingual Matters.

Pavlenko, A. (2008). Emotion and emotion-laden words in the bilingual lexicon. *Bilingualism: Language and Cognition, 11*(2), 147–164.

Perović, S., & Vuković-Stanatović, M. (2021). Universality and cultural variation in the conceptualisation of *love* via metaphors, metonymies and cultural scripts: The case of Montenegrin. *Círculo de Lingüística Aplicada a la Comunicación, 85*, 45–60.

Phan, K. L., Wager, T., Taylor, S. F., & Liberzon, I. (2002). Functional neuroanatomy of emotion: A meta-analysis of emotion activation studies in PET and fMRI. *NeuroImage, 16*(2), 331–348.

Plamper, J. (2015). *The history of emotions: An introduction.* Oxford: Oxford University Press.

Plutchik, R. (1962). *The emotions: Facts, theories, and a new model.* New York: Random House.

Plutchik, R. (1980). *Emotion: A psychoevolutionary synthesis.* New York: Harper & Row.

Plutchik, R. (2001). The nature of emotions. *American Scientist, 89*(4), 344–350.

Plutchik, R. (2003). *Emotions and life: Perspectives from psychology, biology, and evolution.* Washington, DC: American Psychological Association.

Plutchik, R., & Conte, H. R. (Eds.). (1997). *Circumplex models of personality and emotions.* Washington, DC: American Psychological Association.

Ponsonnet, M. (2022). Emotional linguistic relativity and cross-cultural research. In Schiewer, Alatarriba, & Ng, *Language and emotion*, 2:1033–1061.

Posner, J., Russell, J. A., & Peterson, B. S. (2005). The circumplex model of affect: An integrative approach to affective neuroscience, cognitive development, and psychopathology. *Development and Psychopathology, 17*(3), 715–734.

Power, M. J., & Dalgleish, T. (2015). *Cognition and emotion: From order to disorder.* 3rd ed. New York: Psychology Press.

Printz, J. J. (2004). *Gut feelings: A perceptual theory of emotion.* Oxford: Oxford University Press.

Pritzker, S. E., Fenigsen, J., & Wilce, J. M. (Eds.). (2020). *The Routledge handbook of language and emotion.* New York: Routledge.

Quinn, N., & Mathews, H. F. (2016). Emotional arousal in the making of cultural selves. *Anthropological Theory, 16*(4), 359–389.

Ratner, C. (1989). A social constructionist critique of the naturalistic theory of emotion. *The Journal of Mind and Behavior, 10*(3), 211–230.

Raz, G., Touroutoglou, A., Wilson-Mendenhall, C., et al. (2016). Functional connectivity dynamics during film viewing reveal common networks for different emotional experiences. *Cognitive, Affective, and Behavioral Neuroscience, 16*(4), 709–723.

Reddy, W. M. (1997). Against constructionism: The historical ethnography of emotions. *Current Anthropology, 38*(3), 327–351.

Reddy, W. M. (2001). *The navigation of feeling.* Cambridge: Cambridge University Press.

Reddy, W. M. (2009). Historical research on the self and emotions. *Emotion Review, 1*(4), 302–315.

Reddy, W. M. (2020). The unavoidable intentionality of affect: The history of emotions and the neurosciences of the present day. *Emotion Review, 12*(3), 168–178.

Riemer, N. (2006). Reductive paraphrase and meaning: A critique of Wierzbickian semantics. *Linguistics and Philosophy, 29*(3), 347–379.

Rolls, E. T. (1999). *The brain and emotion.* Oxford: Oxford University Press.

Rolls, E. T. (2017). Evolution of the emotional brain. In S. Watanabe, M. A. Hofman, & T. Shimizu (Eds.), *Evolution of the brain, cognition, and emotion in vertebrates* (pp. 251–272). Tokyo: Springer.

Romania, V. (2022). Vilfredo Pareto. In C. Cerulo, & A. Scribano (Eds.), *The emotions in the classics of sociology: A study in social theory* (pp. 96–112). New York: Routledge.

Romney, A. K., Moore, C. C., & Rusch, C. D. (1997). Cultural universals: Measuring the semantic structure of emotion terms in English and Japanese. *Proceedings of the National Academy of Sciences, 94*(10), 5489–5494.

Rorty, A. O. (1980). Introduction. In A. O. Rorty (Ed.), *Explaining emotions* (pp. 1–9). Berkeley: University of California Press.

Rosaldo, M. Z. (1980). *Knowledge and passion: Ilongot notions of self & social life.* Cambridge: Cambridge University Press.

Rosaldo, M. Z. (1984). Toward an anthropology of self and feeling. In Shweder, & LeVine, *Culture theory*, pp. 137–157.

Rosaldo, R. (1984). Grief and a headhunter's rage: On the cultural force of emotions. In E. M. Bruner (Ed.), *Text, play, and story: The construction and reconstruction of self and society* (pp. 178–195). Washington, DC: American Ethnological Society.

Roseman, I. J. (1984). Cognitive determinants of emotion: A structural theory. *Review of Personality and Social Psychology, 5*, 11–36.

Roseman, I. J. (2011). Emotional behaviors, emotivational goals, emotion strategies: Multiple levels of organization integrate variable and consistent responses. *Emotion Review, 3*(4), 434–443.

Roseman, I. J. (2013). Appraisal in the emotion system: Coherence in strategies for coping. *Emotion Review, 5*(2), 141–149.

Rosenwein, B. H. (2001). Writing without fear about early medieval emotions. *Early Medieval Europe, 10*(2), 229–234.

Rosenwein, B. H. (2010). Problems and methods in the history of emotions. *Passions in Context, 1*, 1–30.

Rosenwein, B. H. (2016). *Generations of feeling: A history of emotions, 600–1700.* Cambridge: Cambridge University Press.

Rosenwein, B. H. (2021). Emotions: Some historical observations. *History of Psychology, 24*(2), 107–111.

Rosenwein, B. H., & Cristiani, R. (2017). *What is the history of emotion?* Cambridge: Polity Press.

Roughley, N. (Ed.). (2000). *Being humans: Anthropological universality and particularity in transdisciplinary perspectives.* Berlin: Walter se Gruter.

Rubin, B. P. (2009). Changing brains: The emergence of the field of adult neurogenesis. *BioSocieties, 4*, 407–424.

Russell, J. A. (1979). Affective space is bipolar. *Journal of Personality and Social Psychology, 37*(3), 345–356.

Russell, J. A. (1980). A circumplex model of affect. *Journal of Personality and Social Psychology, 39*(6), 1161–1178.

Russell, J. A. (1991). Culture and the categorization of emotions. *Psychological Bulletin, 110*(3), 426–450.

Russell, J. A. (1994). Is there universal recognition of emotion from facial expression? A review of the cross-cultural studies. *Psychological Bulletin, 115*(1), 102–141.

Russell, J. A. (2009). Emotion, core affect, and psychological construction. *Cognition and Emotion, 23*(7), 1259–1283.

Russell, J. A., & Barrett, L. F. (1999). Core affect, prototypical emotional episodes, and other things called emotion: Dissecting the elephant. *Journal of Personality and Social Psychology, 76*(5), 805–819.

Russell, J. A., & Fehr, B. (1987). Relativity in the perception of emotion in facial expressions. *Journal of Experimental Psychology: General, 116*(3), 223–237.

Russell, J. A., & Fehr, B. (1994). Fuzzy concepts in a fuzzy hierarchy: Varieties of anger. *Journal of Personality and Social Psychology, 67*(2), 186–205.

Russell, J. A., & Fernández-Dols, J. M. (1997). What does a facial expression mean? In J. A. Russell, & J. M. Fernández-Dols (Eds.), *The psychology of facial expression* (pp. 1–30). Cambridge: Cambridge University Press.

Saarimäki, H., Gotsopoulos, A., Jääskeläinen, I. P., et al. (2016). Discrete neural signatures of basic emotions. *Cerebral Cortex, 26*(6), 2563–2573.

Saarimäki, H., Ejtehadian, L. F., Glerean, E., et al. (2018). Distributed affective space represents multiple emotion categories across the human brain. *Social Cognitive and Affective Neuroscience, 13*(5), 471–482.

Saarimäki, H., Glerean, E., Smirnov, D., et al. (2022). Classification of emotion categories based on functional connectivity patterns of the human brain. *NeuroImage, 247*, article 118800.

Santos, D., & Maia, B. (2018). Language, emotion, and the emotions: A computational introduction. *Language and Linguistics Compass, 12*(6), article e12279.

Sapir, E. (1921). *Language, an introduction to the study of speech.* New York: Harcourt Brace.

Satpute, A. B., & Lindquist, K. A. (2021). At the neural intersection between language and emotion. *Affective Science, 2*(2), 207–220.

Saucier, G., Thalmayer, A. G., & Bel-Bahar, T. S. (2014). Human attribute concepts: Relative ubiquity across twelve mutually isolated languages. *Journal of Personality and Social Psychology, 107*(1), 199–216.

Sauter, D. A., & Russell, J. A. (2024). What do nonverbal expressions tell us about emotion? In Scarantino, *Emotion theory*, pp. 543–560.

Sauter, D. A., Eisner, F., Ekman, P., & Scott, S. K. (2010). Cross-cultural recognition of basic emotions through nonverbal emotional vocalizations. *PNAS, 107*(6), 2408–2412.

Sauter, D. A., Eisner, F., Ekman, P., & Scott, S. K. (2015). Emotional vocalizations are recognized across cultures regardless of the valence of distractors. *Psychological Science, 26*(3), 354–356.

Scarantino, A. (2009). Core affect and natural affective kinds. *Philosophy of Science, 76*(5), 940–957.

Scarantino, A. (2012a). Discrete emotions: From folk psychology to causal mechanisms. In P. Zachar, & R. D. Ellis (Eds.), *Categorical versus dimensional models of affect: A seminar on the theories of Panksepp and Russell* (pp. 135–154). Amsterdam: John Benjamins.

Scarantino, A. (2012b). How to define emotions scientifically. *Emotion Review, 4*(4), 358–368.

Scarantino, A. (2012c). Functional specialization does not require a one-to-one mapping between brain regions and emotions. *Behavioral and Brain Science, 35*(3), 161–162.

Scarantino, A. (2014). The motivational theory of emotions. In J. D'arms, & D. Jacobson (Eds.), *Moral psychology and human agency: Philosophical essays on the science of ethics* (pp. 156–185). Oxford: Oxford University Press.

Scarantino, A. (2015). Basic emotions, psychological construction, and the problem of variability. In L. F. Barrett, & J. A. Russell (Eds.), *The psychological construction of emotion* (pp. 334–376). New York: Guilford.

Scarantino, A. (2016). The philosophy of emotion and its impact on affective science. In Barrett, Lewis, & Haviland-Jones, *Handbook of emotions*, pp. 3–48.

Scarantino, A. (2018). Are LeDoux's survival circuits basic emotions under a different name? *Current Opinion in Behavioral Sciences, 24*, 75–82.

Scarantino, A. (Ed.). (2024). *Emotion theory: The Routledge comprehensive guide*. 2 vols. New York: Routledge.

Scarantino, A., & de Sousa, R. (2018). Emotion. In E. Zalta (Ed.), *Stanford encyclopedia of philosophy*. https://plato.stanford.edu/entries/emotion/.

Scarantino, A., & Griffiths, P. (2011). Don't give up on basic emotions. *Emotion Review, 3*(4), 444–454.

Schachter, S., & Singer, J. (1962). Cognitive, social and physiological determinants of emotional state. *Psychological Review, 69*(5), 379–399.

Scherer, K. R. (1984). Emotion as a multicomponent process: A model and some cross-cultural data. *Review of Personality & Social Psychology, 5*, 37–63.

Scherer, K. R. (1994). Toward a concept of "modal emotions." In P. Ekman, & R. J. Davidson (Eds.), *The nature of emotion: Fundamental questions* (pp. 25–31). Oxford: Oxford University Press.

Scherer, K. R. (1997). The role of culture in emotion-antecedent appraisal. *Journal of Personality and Social Psychology, 73*(5), 902–922.

Scherer, K. R. (2001). Appraisal considered as a process of multilevel sequential checking. In K. R. Scherer, A. Schorr, & T. Johnstone (Eds.), *Appraisal processes in emotion: Theory, methods, research* (pp. 92–120). Oxford: Oxford University Press.

Scherer, K. R. (2009a). Modal emotions. In R. J. Davidson, K. R. Scherer, & H. H. Goldsmith (Eds.), *Handbook of affective sciences* (pp. 257–258). Oxford: Oxford University Press.

Scherer, K. R. (2009b). The dynamic architecture of emotion: Evidence for the component process model. *Cognition and Emotion, 23*(7), 1307–1351.

Scherer, K. R., & Moors, A. (2019). The emotion process: Event appraisal and component differentiation. *Annual Review of Psychology, 70*, 719–745.

Schiewer, G. L., Altarriba, J., & Ng, B. C. (Eds.). (2022–2023). *Language and emotion: An international handbook*. 3 vols. Berlin: De Gruyter.

Schnell, R. (2021). *Histories of emotion: Modern-premodern*. Berlin: De Gruyter.

Scott, B. (2019). *Affective disorders: Emotion in colonial and postcolonial literature*. Liverpool: Liverpool University Press.

Sedgwick, E. K., & Frank, A. (1995). Shame in the cybernetic fold: Reading Silvan Tomkins. *Critical Inquiry, 21*(2), 496–522.

Sell, A., Tooby, J., & Cosmides, L. (2009). Formidability and the logic of human anger. *PNAS, 106*(35), 15073–15078.

Semin, G. R. (2012). Balancing emotions between constraints and construction: Comment on Boiger and Mesquita. *Emotion Review, 4*(3), 230–231.

Shakuf, V., Ben-David, B., Wegner, T. G. G., et al. (2022). Processing emotional prosody in a foreign language: The case of German and Hebrew. *Journal of Cultural Cognitive Studies, 6*(3), 251–268.

Shaver, P., Schwartz, J., Kirson, D., & O'Connor, C. (1987). Emotion knowledge: Further exploration of a prototype approach. *Journal of Personality and Social Psychology, 52*(6), 1061–1086.

Shaver, P. R., Wu, S., & Schwartz, J. C. (1992). Cross-cultural similarities and differences in emotion and its representation: A prototype approach. *Review of Personality and Social Psychology, 13*, 175–212.

Shiota, M. N. (2024). Basic and discrete emotion theories. In Scarantino, *Emotion theory*, pp. 310–330.

Shiota, M. N., Camras, L. A., & Adolphs, R. (2023). The future of affective science: Introduction to the special issue. *Affective Science, 4*(3), 429–442.

Shore, B. (1996). *Culture in mind: Cognition, culture, and the problem of meaning*. Oxford: Oxford University Press.

Shore, B. (2000). Human diversity and human nature: The life and times of a false dichotomy. In Roughley, *Being humans*, pp. 81–104.

Shott, S. (1979). Emotion and social life: A symbolic interactionist analysis. *American Journal of Sociology, 84*(6), 1317–1334.

Shweder, R. A. (1990). Cultural psychology – what is it? In J. W. Stigler, R. A. Shweder, & G. Herdt (Eds.), *Cultural psychology: Essays on comparative human development* (pp. 1–44). Cambridge: Cambridge University Press.

Shweder, R. A. (1991). *Thinking through cultures: Expeditions in cultural psychology*. Cambridge, MA: Harvard University Press.

Shweder, R. A. (2004). Deconstructing the emotions for the sake of comparative research. In A. S. R. Manstead, N. Frijda, & A. Fischer (Eds.), *Feelings and emotions: The Amsterdam symposium* (pp. 81–97). Cambridge: Cambridge University Press.

Shweder, R. A. (2007). An anthropological perspective: The revival of cultural psychology – Some premonitions and reflections. In S. Kitayama, & D. Cohen (Eds.), *Handbook of cultural psychology* (pp. 821–836). New York: Guilford.

Shweder, R. A., & LeVine, R. A. (Eds.). (1984). *Culture theory: Essays on mind, self, and emotion*. Cambridge: Cambridge University Press.

Siegel, E. H., Sands, M. K., Van den Noortgate, W., et al. (2018). Emotion fingerprints or emotion populations? A meta-analytic investigation of autonomic features of emotion categories. *Psychological Bulletin*, *144*(4), 343–393.

Sinha, D. (2002). Culture and psychology: Perspectives of cross-cultural psychology. *Psychology and Developing Societies*, *14*(1), 11–25.

Singh, M. (2021). The sympathetic plot, its psychological origins, and implications for the evolution of fiction. *Emotion Review*, *13*(3), 183–198.

Smaldino, P. E., & Schank, J. C. (2012). Invariants of human emotion. *Behavioral Brain Science*, *35*(3), 164.

Smith-Lovin, L., & Winkielman, P. (2010). The social psychologies of emotion: A bridge that is not too far. *Social Psychology Quarterly*, *73*(4), 327–332.

Solomon, R. C. (1984). Getting angry: The Jamesian theory of emotion in anthropology. In Shweder, & LeVine, *Culture theory*, pp. 238–256.

Solomon, R. C. (1995). The cross-cultural comparison of emotion. In J. Marks, & R. T. Ames, (Eds.), *Emotions in Asian thought* (pp. 253–294). Albany: State University of New York Press.

Solomon, R. C. (2002). Back to basics: On the very idea of "basic emotions." *Journal for the Theory of Social Behaviour*, *32*(2), 115–144.

Solomon, R. C. (Ed.). (2004). *Thinking about feeling: Contemporary philosophers on emotions*. Oxford: Oxford University Press.

Spencer, D., & Davies, J. (Eds.). (2010). *Anthropological fieldwork: A relational process*. Newcastle Upon Tyne: Cambridge Scholars.

Spiro, M. E. (1984). Some reflections on cultural determinism and relativism with special reference to emotion and reason. In Shweder, & LeVine, *Culture theory*, pp. 323–346.

Stets, J. E. (2010). Future directions in the sociology of emotion. *Emotion Review*, *2*(3), 265–268.

Stets, J. E. (2012). Current emotion research in sociology: Advances in the discipline. *Emotion Review*, *4*(3), 326–334.

Stets, J. E., & Turner, J. H. (Eds.). (2006). *The handbook of the sociology of emotions*. New York: Springer.

Stets, J. E., & Turner, J. H. (2008). The sociology of emotion. In M. Lewis, J. M. Haviland-Jones, & L. F. Barrett (Eds.), *The handbook of emotion, third edition* (pp. 32–46). New York: Guilford.

Stets, J. E., & Turner, J. H. (Eds.). (2014). *Handbook of the sociology of emotions: Volume II*. Dordrecht: Springer.

Stodulka, T. (2017). Towards an integrative anthropology of emotion: A case study from Yogyakarta. In A. Storch (Ed.), *Consensus and dissent: Negotiating emotion in the public space* (pp. 9–34). Amsterdam: John Benjamins.

Stodulka, T., Selim, N., & Mattes, D. (2018). Affective scholarship: Doing anthropology with epistemic affects. *Ethos*, *46*(4), 519–536.

Stodulka, T., Dinkelaker, S., & Thajib, F. (Eds.). (2019). *Affective dimensions of fieldwork and ethnography.* New York: Springer.

Sundararajan, L. (2015). *Understanding emotion in Chinese culture.* New York: Springer.

Svašek, M. (2005). Introduction: Emotions in anthropology. In K. Milton, & M. Svašek (Eds.), *Mixed emotions: Anthropological studies of feeling* (pp. 1–23). Oxford: Oxford University Press.

Tappolet, C. (2023). *Philosophy of emotion: A contemporary introduction.* New York: Routledge.

Taylor, H. (2020). Emotions, concepts and the indeterminacy of natural kinds. *Synthese, 197*(5), 2073–2093.

Tepora, T. (2020). What, if anything, can the history of emotions learn from the neurosciences? *Cultural History, 9*(1), 93–105.

Thamm, R. (2004). Towards a universal power and status theory of emotion. *Advances in Group Processes, 21,* 189–222.

Thoits, P. A. (1985). Self-labeling processes in mental illness: The role of emotional deviance. *American Journal of Sociology, 91*(2), 221–249.

Thoits, P. A. (1989). The sociology of emotions. *Annual Review of Sociology, 15,* 317–342.

Tissari, H. (2017). Current emotion research in English linguistics: Words for emotions in the history of English. *Emotion Review, 9*(1), 86–94.

Tomkins, S. (1962). *Affect, imagery, consciousness. Vol 1: The positive affects.* New York: Springer.

Tooby, J. (2020). Evolutionary psychology as the crystalizing core of a unified modern social science. *Evolutionary Behavioral Sciences, 14*(4), 390–403.

Tooby, J., & Cosmides, L. (1990a). The past explains the present: Emotional adaptations and the structure of ancestral environments. *Ethology and Sociobiology, 11*(4–5), 375–424.

Tooby, J., & Cosmides, L. (1990b). On the universality of human nature and the uniqueness of the individual: The role of genetics and adaptation. *Journal of Personality, 58*(1), 17–67.

Tooby, J., & Cosmides, L. (2008). The evolutionary psychology of the emotions and their relationship to internal regulatory variables. In M. Lewis, J. M. Haviland-Jones, & L. F. Barrett (Eds.), *The handbook of emotion, third edition* (pp. 114–137). New York: Guilford.

Tooby, J., & Cosmides, L. (2015). The theoretical foundations of evolutionary psychology. In D. M. Buss (Ed.), *The handbook of evolutionary psychology: Foundations* (pp. 3–87). New York: John Wiley.

Touroutoglou, A., Lindquist, K. A., Dickerson, B. C., & Barrett, L. F. (2015). Intrinsic connectivity in the human brain does not reveal networks for "basic" emotions. *Social Cognitive and Affective Neuroscience, 10*(9), 1257–1265.

Tracy, J. L. (2014). An evolutionary approach to understanding distinct emotions. *Emotion Review, 6*(4), 308–312.

Tsai, J. L., Chentsova-Dutton, Y., Freire-Bebeau, L., & Przymus, D. E. (2002). Emotional expression and physiology in European Americans and Hmong Americans. *Emotion, 2*(4), 380–397.

Turner, J. H. (1996). The evolution of emotions in humans: A Darwinian-Durkheimian analysis. *Journal for the Theory of Social Behaviour, 26*(1), 1–33.

Turner, J. H. (1999). Toward a general sociological theory of emotions. *Journal for the Theory of Social Behaviour, 29*(2), 133–161.

Turner, J. H. (2000). *On the origins of human emotions: A sociological inquiry into the evolution of human affect.* Stanford: Stanford University Press.

Turner, J. H. (2002). *Face to face: Toward a sociological theory of interpersonal behavior.* Stanford: Stanford University Press.

Turner, J. H. (2007). *Human emotions: A sociological theory.* New York: Routledge.

Turner, J. H. (2021). *On human nature: The biology and sociology of what made us human.* New York: Routledge.

Turner, J. H., & Stets, J. E. (2005). *The sociology of emotion.* Cambridge: Cambridge University Press.

Turner, V. (1967). *The forest of symbols: Aspects of Ndembu ritual.* Ithaca: Cornell University Press.

Vick, S. - J., Waller, B. M., Parr, L. A., Smith Pasqualini, M. C., & Bard, K. A. (2007). A cross-species comparison of facial morphology and movement in humans and chimpanzees using the Facial Action Coding System (FACS). *Journal of Nonverbal Behavior, 31*(1), 1–20.

Vytal, K., & Hamann, S. (2010). Neuroimaging support for discrete neural correlates of basic emotions: A voxel-based meta-analysis. *Journal of Cognitive Neuroscience, 22*(12), 2864–2885.

Wager, T. D., Kang, J., Johnson, T. D., et al. (2015). A Bayesian model of category-specific emotional brain responses. *PLos Computational Biology, 11*(4), article e1004066.

Watzl, S. (2019). Culture or biology? If this sounds interesting, you might be confused. In J. Valsiner (Ed.), *Social philosophy of science for the social sciences* (pp. 45–71). Cham: Springer.

Weissbourd, E. (2023). Shakespeare from the bottom: Transnationalism, unfounded whiteness, and the First Folio. *Shakespeare Quarterly, 74*(3), 204–216.

Wetherell, M. (2012). *Affect and emotion: A new social science understanding.* Los Angeles: Sage.

Whorf, B. L. (1956). *Language, thought, and reality: Selected writings of Benjamin Lee Whorf.* Cambridge, MA: The MIT Press.

Wierzbicka, A. (1986). Human emotions: Universal or cultural-specific? *American Anthropologist, 88*(3), 584–594.

Wierzbicka, A. (1992). *Semantics, culture, and cognition: Universal human concepts in culture-specific configurations.* Oxford: Oxford University Press.

Wierzbicka, A. (1996). *Semantics: Primes and universals.* Oxford: Oxford University Press.

Wierzbicka, A. (1998). "Sadness" and "anger" in Russian: The non-universality of the so-called "basic human emotions." In A. Athanasiadou, & E. Tabakowska (Eds.), Speaking of emotions: Conceptualisation and expression (pp. 3–28). Berlin: De Gruyter.

Wierzbicka, A. (1999). *Emotions across languages and cultures: Diversity and universals.* Cambridge: Cambridge University Press.

Wierzbicka, A. (2009). Language and metalanguage: Key issues in emotion research. *Emotion Review, 1*(1), 3–14.

Wierzbicka, A. (2014). *Imprisoned in English: The hazards of English as a default language.* Oxford: Oxford University Press.

Wilce, J. M. (2009). *Language and emotion.* Cambridge: Cambridge University Press.

Wilce, J. M. (2014). Current emotion research in linguistic anthropology. *Emotion Review, 6*(1), 77–85.

Wilkowski, B. M., Meier, B. P., Robinson, M. D., Carter, M. S., & Feltman, R. (2009). "Hot-headed" is more than an expression: The embodied representation of anger in terms of heat. *Emotion, 9*(4), 464–477.

Wilson-Mendenhall, C. D., Barrett, L. F., & Barsalou, L. W. (2013). Neural evidence that human emotions share core affective properties. *Psychological Science, 24*(6), 947–956.

Winter, B., & Matlock, T. (2017). Primary metaphors are both cultural and embodied. In B. Hampe (Ed.), *Metaphor: Embodied cognition and discourse* (pp. 99–115). Cambridge: Cambridge University Press.

Witkower, Z., Hill, A. K., Koster, J., & Tracy, J. L. (2021). Beyond face value: Evidence for the universality of bodily expressions of emotion. *Affective Science, 2*(3), 221–229.

Witkower, Z., Rule, N. O., & Tracy, J. L. (2023). Emotions do reliably co-occur with predicted facial signals. Comment on Durán and Fernández-Dols (2021). *Emotion, 23*(3), 903–907.

Wnuk, E., & Ito, Y. (2021). The heart's downward path to happiness: Cross-cultural diversity in spatial metaphors of affect. *Cognitive Linguistics*, *32*(2), 195–218.

Wojciehowski, H., & Gallese, V. (2011). How stories make us feel: Toward an embodied narratology. *California Italian Studies*, *2*(1), https://escholarship.org/uc/item/3jg726c2.

Wojciehowski, H., & Gallese, V. (2018). Narrative and the biocultural turn. *Costellazioni*, *5*, 9–21.

Wojciehowski, H., & Gallese, V. (2022). Embodiment: Embodied simulation and emotional engagement with fictional characters. In Hogan, Irish, & Hogan, *Routledge companion*, pp. 61–73.

Wood, A., & Coan, J. A. (2023). Beyond nature versus nurture: The emergence of emotion. *Affective Science*, *4*(3), 443–452.

Ye, Z. (2001). An inquiry into "sadness" in Chinese. In J. Harkins, & A. Wierzbicka (Eds.), *Emotions in crosslinguistic perspective* (pp. 359–404). Berlin: De Gruyter.

Zeng, Y. (2022). Universality in Emily Brontë's "remembrance." *Advances in Literary Study*, *10*(4), 313–320.

Zhou, F., Zhao, W., Qi, Z., et al. (2021). A distributed fMRI-based signature for the subjective experience of fear. *Nature Communications*, *12*(1), article 6643.

Zunshine, L. (Ed.). (2015). *The Oxford handbook of cognitive literary studies*. Oxford: Oxford University Press.

# Acknowledgments

Though the faults of this Element are all mine, I have benefited enormously from the help of other scholars in putting it together. I am grateful to Katie Barclay, Andrew Beatty, Rob Boddice, Giovanna Colombetti, Agnes Moors, Brian Parkinson, Jerry Parrott, Andrea Scarantino, and Christine Tappolet, as well as to the (many) authors who so generously shared their forthcoming publications with me. Much is also owed to Ken Keith, the manuscript's anonymous reviewer, and the CUP team for all they've done to bring this manuscript into the world. As always, my work would not be possible without the support of my family.

*Finally, this Element is dedicated to Lani Shiota and*
*Patrick Hogan – the two people who have taught me the*
*most about emotion, and two people who I feel absolutely*
*blessed to have in my life.*

# Cambridge Elements ⁼

# Psychology and Culture

### Kenneth D. Keith
*University of San Diego*
Kenneth D. Keith is author or editor of more than 160 publications on cross-cultural psychology, quality of life, intellectual disability, and the teaching of psychology. He was the 2017 president of the Society for the Teaching of Psychology.

## About the Series
Elements in Psychology and Culture features authoritative surveys and updates on key topics in cultural, cross-cultural, and indigenous psychology. Authors are internationally recognized scholars whose work is at the forefront of their subdisciplines within the realm of psychology and culture.

# Cambridge Elements ☰

# Psychology and Culture

## Elements in the Series

A full series listing is available at: www.cambridge.org/EPAC

Printed in the United States
by Baker & Taylor Publisher Services